BEST BREAKUP EVER!

Best Breakup Ever!

Bouncing back from your breakup
with **humor** and **dignity**

by **April Hirschman**

Published by *Magickal Times Books*

Book & Cover Design by Sofía Limón
All Photos of Author by Lydia Daniller
Illustrations by April Hirschman

ISBN-978-0-9979416-3-0

For Grandma Muriel

Thank you for the inheritance of laughter and joie de vivre.
I miss you every single day.

My old self refuses to die. The new is struggling to be reborn. In this interim a great variety of morbid symptoms appear.

Jeff in Venice, Death in Varanasi, Geoff Dyer

That is to say: I have been trying to go limp in the face of my heartache, as another friend says he does in the face of his anxiety. *Think of it as an act of civil disobedience,* he says. *Let the police peel you up.*

Bluets, Maggie Nelson

If you don't want us to be apart, then don't ever leave me.

My 3-year-old niece

I wish you would take up golf.

A recent text from my first girlfriend

Safely Yourself Again 12
How to Hop Through These Pages

In The Beginning: What to Expect When You're Despairing 19
Your Breakup Tool Kit
Clearing Responsibilities at Work
All About Eating
Two Occasions: Day and Night
Breakup Math
Coming Off The Love Drug

Sex After Ex 34
The Best Way to Get Over Somebody is to Get Under Somebody Else
Put Your Hands on Me

Kelp from Your Friends 39
I Get By With a Little Kelp from My Friends
Friday, I'm in Love
Let Us Go to the Dogs Tonight
Adult Aid

Feeling the Feelings 47
The Stages of Breakup Recovery
No More I Love Yous
I Hate You I Love You
Building The Mystery
Back is Forward
Will You Remeber Me?
If Only
If I Cry In Your Shower

In The Middle: What to Expect When You're Still Despairing 57
Mood Kickstarters
The Breakup Ritual: A Knife and Five Cranberries

Always Look on The Bright Side of Life 64
Here's Why I'm Better Without You
Through a Lens, Darkly
Night Moves
That Spring in Your Step
Pronoia

Get Out There! 71
Breakfast at Tiffany's
Movers and Shakers
Give Back
The Geographic Cure
Doing What Comes Natur'lly

Fire Your Critic and Hire Stevie Nicks 81
Your Inner Critic Sucks
Stevie Nicks, The Sun, and You
Your Wiseass Older Self
But Everybody Loves You

Castles Made of Sand 90
The Tower
The Lost House
The Never Not Broken Goddess

Your Self-Love Nest 96
Aphrodite Said So
Space Speaks
Happy Basket

Unusual and Usual Recovery Tips 104
Just Float
And Stay Obsessed
The Fever of Creation
Movie Therapy
Oracle All About It
Breakup Coaching
Bridal Dress Therapy

Your Playlist and Other Musical Things 128
Five Easy Pieces
Jealousy
You Can't Take That Away From Me

Radical Self-Care 136
Treat Yo'self
Acupuncture Points for Heart Healing
Your Hair Journey

Thoughts! Journals! Mantras! 143
It's All in the Telling
The Diary of You
Let's Mantra Again Like We Did Last Summer
Eternal Sunshine of the Spotless Mind
The Best Letter You Never Sent
Can You Picture This?

In The End: What to Expect When You're Bouncing Back! **154**

Love the One You're With **155**

The Lover Who Never Leaves You
Like the Sky Holds the Earth
The You In You
The Power of One

Close Encounters of the Ex Kind **164**

Wanting Contact (with you)
Is Social Media Stalking for You?
Hug and Release

Better Luck Next Time **171**

The Thesis Statement is True

And Now Back to Me **174**

New Rules
Everybody, Lives Back!
Remembering the Beginning

Goodbye for Now **177**

The Past Loves Bush
No Bummer Future Thinking
Every Single Breath

BONUS SECTION **182**

Recipes: The Heart Healing Kitchen
Books, Movies, TV
Resource Guide
April's Offerings

Safely Yourself Again

I did not lose myself all at once. I rubbed out my face over the years washing away my pain, the same way carvings on stone are worn down by water.

Amy Tan

Welcome home. You have traveled a lonely road of heartache to get here, through the desert of disappointment. Sit; let me wash your feet with rosewater. Wouldn't that be nice? I know you feel alone in the world, as alone as the *Little Prince* on his tiny planet in the cosmos. But you have companions in this temple. Come inside. See the velvet, brocade, and satin fabrics that line the cool walls? See how the skylights catch the jewels hanging from the ceiling? We got you. And you got this. This book and me, your Temple Priestess and Life Coach. We are all here for you. Come weary traveler. Come tell us your story.

What does it mean to be "Safely Yourself Again?" It doesn't mean that you were unsafe in your last relationship, at least I hope not! In fact, you were probably opening up and making yourself vulnerable, which is great. What it means is that you are off the delightful roller coaster of a romantic relationship. The ego has landed. You are not constantly relating to another being, your partner. And once again you are alone with your thoughts and who you are. You are different when you're in relationship—always planning your life around another. Maybe you had a partner who really got you to go out and do things you wouldn't normally do, as in traveling to Zanzibar and playing ice hockey. Or perhaps you abandoned very important parts of yourself in your last ride on the love train.

Maybe you can't wait for a greasy burger now that the beautiful vegan dumped you. Or perhaps your ex always wanted to stay in and Netflix and Chill while you wanted to get down on the dance floor.

In the movie adaptation of *Eat, Pray, Love,* Julia Roberts plays the author's character. She is a chameleon whose shape shifts with each partner. If they wear a leather jacket, so does she, modeling subconscious ways we accommodate the needs of others by changing ourselves.

I have a morning ritual that grounds me. I make my bed, meditate for a few minutes, do a little yoga, belly dance, brush my hair, write in my Julia-Cameron-inspired Morning Pages journal, and check my schedule. It sounds elaborate, but it's actually quick and lovely. It's often the best part of my day. It's the time I am with myself, my thoughts, breathing, centering, and moving my body. Our rituals are often the first to go in a relationship. When I'm in a relationship it's hard to make time for all this. I'm a cuddle fiend with a high sex drive. I'd rather be in bed with my babe than doing anything else.

I don't quit my morning ritual altogether, I just do it less and find myself less centered. What routines have you abandoned that you can return to? What rituals were interrupted? Did your ex hate it when you practiced the piano? Did they always want to go out to eat, thus missing out on your culinary sensations?

Sometimes the stakes are even higher in what we abdicated. Perhaps you had to forgo your love of kink, that you're non-monogamous at heart, or that you're more soulful and quiet while your ex was loud and wild. Maybe you're bisexual, but your boyfriend told you that you were straight/gay because you were dating him. Maybe you stopped dancing or maybe you stopped dreaming. I know you probably don't feel like dreaming right now about your big, wide-open, all-possible future. But it's there all the same. And you are at its center—the unquestioned STAR of the show. How about just making a list of three things you are gaining from being safely yourself again. Or just say them aloud to yourself right now.

There's only one thing that will help you get over a breakup... Time! You can close the book now...no...wait! Though that statement is kind of true, as precious time is passing, you will still need to breathe (in and out), to eat (about three times a day...I know, I know!), and to be alive. And hopefully during some of that time, you will THRIVE. Is it possible? Yes, it is. That you have this book in your hands is already impressive. That you went to the library or a bookstore or Amazon or slipped it off your sister's shelf when she wasn't looking is badass. You are on the path to thriving.

Let's join together in the Temple of Healing. Just because you are reading this book alone in the loft of your yurt doesn't mean you are alone. You can invite whomever you like to help you on this journey. We are all going through losses all the time; for some their lease is up, others have lost a loved one, still others lost their job. You are not alone.

I'm here. Your ancestors are here, waiting patiently for you to offer them a chair. Not that rickety one by the fireplace; your ancestors are old! Give them the cushy chairs.

Let's be in this together. Though we may feel our most lonely after a breakup, it actually unites us with the world of people who have also been through this: acrobats in Indonesia, feminists in Canada, and lounge singers in India.

I wrote this because when I was recovering from a breakup I didn't find the book I needed. I wanted to open up the pages to a sensitive, funny friend who knew what I was going through. I wanted to be inspired to laugh and cry. I didn't want a detached therapist voice speaking from a cloud as if they knew all the answers. I wanted someone down digging in the mud with me.

I didn't always want the overly tender, precious self-help books like *When Things Fall Apart* by Pema Chödrön. The title itself implies a certain dreariness that's just a tad on the nose for folks feeling down and out. Note: I love Pema Chödrön! She's the bee's knees. Her insights have rearranged my perspectives on life for the better. At one time, her book was right for me. At another time, it wasn't. Some self-help books seem to exist in a parallel universe wherein we breathe, meditate, contemplate. I can't always dwell in that place via a book. That's why I have included real-life stuff like recipes, movie therapy, and practical suggestions. I want this book to hold your hand in real time, not in an inaccessible, ethereal realm.

While sobbing in the library one day, I desperately grabbed *It's Called a Breakup Because It's Broken*. The cover depicts a pink ice cream carton. Did it mean that ice cream was going to be my pal through this breakup or that I should read the book in lieu of climbing into a tub of ice cream?

The books subtitle is: "The smart girl's breakup buddy." This intrinsically divisive phrase exclaims that if you don't read it, you're a stupid girl, but if you do read it, you are leaving your stupid girlfriends in the dust. It's hard to locate any feminist or intersectional consciousness in this snappy phrase. Despite all these red flags, in my despair, I still took it home with me.

It's written by a married couple, the Behrendts, who also wrote the equally condescending *He's Just Not That Into You*, which I can only conclude was written for the so-called "stupid girls." I appreciate their effort and marketing niche, but the breakup book was very heteronormative, targeted women with impulse control issues, and included belittling phrases basically saying, "Chin up, pretty lady." This book brought me no comfort and as a bisexual woman, it left me out of the picture completely. Even as they claimed otherwise, they really smeared their happy marriage in your face. And everyone knows Smug Marrieds are kryptonite to the newly single!

The book in your hands is for people in divorce, but it's also for queer folks, non-traditional folks. It's for people who have never been married, and may never want to be.

HOW TO HOP THROUGH THESE PAGES

I know your breakup won't be "solved" by that trite scene in too many romcoms, where you eat a carton of ice cream while watching a famous romantic movie and sobbing. Neither will it dissipate as you have a night out on the town with your friends, getting wasted off shots of tequila and flirting (or sleeping) with the shady bartender. We're going to take her slow and steady.

You can practice all of the suggestions in this book, some of them, or none at all. Pick and choose the ones that work for you. Even if you don't do any of them, this book will still benefit you by planting good thoughts in your bruised heart. I sometimes get angry at self-help books because they tell me to do things. It's so different from other literary experiences, where I can be passive. I get infuriated when they say in Chapter 6, "Now that you have done all the underwater soul searching in Chapter 5, you are ready to buy a house and fall in love." Am I? But I skipped Chapter 5 (and 4). And just because I am reading your book doesn't mean you know how I am growing or back-stepping.

Sometimes I don't like self-help books if they are too dreary and full of soulful exercises. Why is this little book telling me what to do? You're not the boss of me! On the other hand, some of us like direction and assignments (you know who you are). These are listed under the **Try This** heading at the end of many of the chapters.

As I tell my life coaching clients, there is no coaching formula that works for everyone. There's also no formula to heal from a breakup. That's why this book doesn't follow a pure chronological pattern.

Everyone's journey is different. I've worked with clients through their stages of grief, acting out, and morbid existential angst. I've found that certain common themes and remedies are comforting and healing.

While I was writing this book, my first love contacted me on Facebook. He asked via message: "What happened back in the day to make you stop loving me? I always wondered." I hate the word floored, but I was floored. What a question! How to answer? The message was a big deal, and I wanted to get the answer right. Later that day I heard the Richard Marx song, "Endless Summer Nights."

And I remember how you loved me
Time was all we had until the day we said goodbye
I remember every moment of those endless summer nights.

Like many lyrics, it sounds much better when sung. It's extremely sentimental and it made me think of my hunky first love. He immediately apologized for the message and said I didn't need to answer. But I chose to answer his question. I wrote him a long message back. I had to come to terms with the fact that I was the one to break up with the first love I ever had. Some of that exchange is here in this book, so read on.

I

In The Beginning

WHAT TO EXPECT WHEN YOU'RE DESPAIRING

The formula of happiness and success is just, being actually yourself, in the most vivid possible way you can.

Meryl Streep

Hello, everyone! So glad you made it to this chapter. We will look at what you need support with right away: Work, Food, Day and Night, Sex, Friends, and Feelings. But first you'll get your breakup toolkit. You may be in that part of the heroine/hero's journey where it seems all is lost. But it isn't. Bad stuff went down. That's for sure. But you are just the badass who can bounce back from it with the right focus, tools, and support.

Here's a list of some things that will help you feel comforted and taken care of. There's a hug missing from your life. Let's find some replacements for it. Perhaps these suggestions will spark other ideas for what you need in your toolkit. Some of the tools are described in greater depth further on in the book.

Let's go!

YOUR BREAKUP TOOL KIT

YOUR BED

• Heating pad	• Extra blanket
Being cozy and creating your Nighttime Ritual (see page 67) is important. You may want to add a teddy bear, pet, or special pillow to snuggle up to.	

HAPPY BASKET

• Basket	• Joy-inducing mementos
A Happy Basket is something filled with mementos that bring you joy and comfort, such as photos, cards, and sweet-smelling things (see page 101) for more details about the Happy Basket).	
• Get lost in a dusty, used bookstore. • Ask your friends what they are reading. • Library books are free! Just go to the library or download library books on your device. Bibliotherapists believe that finding the right book to read can be very healing. It doesn't need to be self-help. It could be a children's book, a literary classic, or a nice lesbian vampire trilogy!	

MUSIC

New (or old) music for this new chapter in your life. This is explored more in the chapter titled Five Easy Pieces. (page 128)

SEXY SUPPLIES

• Vibrators	• Coconut oil	• Lubricant	• Sexy Toys
Do you have all the supplies you need? Have you tried coconut oil as a lubricant (when you aren't using condoms)? It's great! Did your ex make off with all the goods? Take yourself on a sex toy buying date.			

JOURNAL OR PILLOW BOOK

• Buy a journal that inspires you to write or start a journal on your computer.
In the chapter The Diary of You (page 144) I go into great detail about this fun self-reflection tool. A journal can be used for the **Try This** sections of the book and for anything else you want to write. Meanwhile, when is the best time to start journaling your thoughts, feelings, fears, joys? Today!

ORACLES

• Tarot Deck	• Angel Cards	• Inspiration Cards
• Bibliomancy (open a book to any page—there's your oracle.) • Street Oracle (things random strangers say or shout at you during the day.) The symbolism, stories, and traditions of the tarot and other oracles will offer guidance about where you are on the journey of healing. See Oracle All About It (page 118) for more information.		

FRIENDS

Just like you need emergency numbers posted on your fridge, you need to know which friends have got your back and when. East Coast/West Coast friend alliances can help you when it's way too early to call a local friend; maybe one on the other coast, or side of the globe, will pick up. Ask your friends if they can be there for you when the red meanies hit.
Which friend can you call at: • 10:00 pm? • 2:00 am? • 7:00 am?

SLEEPOVER PARTIES

• Popcorn	• Movies	• Jammies/Onesies
Arrange a couple of sleepovers with friends either at your house or theirs in the first couple of weeks. You're never too old for a good sleepover.		

SELF-TEXTING OR EMAILING

• Send texts to yourself at night before bed so you can wake up to them.
They can be simple: "Good morning, Gorgeous!" Or you can send long email love letters to yourself. I like this option because self-texts are marked as "read" right away.

ENTERTAINMENT

There's never been an easier time to access shows! You can even get Netflix, Hulu, Amazon, and HBO logins from your siblings/friends.

TREATS IN THE FRIDGE & PANTRY

• Crunchy treats such as crackers and chips	• Sweet treats like healthy cookies, dried fruits	• Smooth treats like kefir, smoothies, and vegan mousse	• Hippie Popcorn (The recipe is on page 191)
Don't stock up on treats and snacks to mindlessly eat yourself into oblivion. Do it as a message that you are thinking of how you want to care for yourself.			

BEAUTIFUL THINGS

• Flowers	• Plants (decorative or live basil or other culinary herbs)	• Baby animal photos. Just look at them. They are so sweet!	• A sketchpad and pens/pencils for spontaneous art making

Okay, now that you have your tool kit, first things first. Let's start with addressing the pressing issues: work, food, sex, and help from friends. Help is on the way!

clearing responsibilities at work

You're not at full capacity right now. And that is okay. There are many strategies for dealing with the responsibilities of life while putting your well-being first.

So let's talk about work. To go or not to go? Some of you might not have a choice, but hopefully you do.

The Possibilities:

1. Go to work, but delay telling anyone until the subject doesn't turn you into the Incredible Crying Person. You can still say "we," wear your wedding ring if you need to, and leave your social media status the same.
   Work can be a good distraction, so for some of you this might be a great way to fill that void that just showed up.
2. You can have "the flu" for three days to a week and be at home. It's all about you right now. There is no right or wrong, just what will make you feel better.
3. If you haven't already taken you-know-who out of your phone, meet up with a friend and have them audit your media as follows: have them clean your phone, Instagram, and Facebook of photos, and your ex boo's phone number. You can also have them put your ex in your phone as an evil emoji. But I really suggest you get that number out of there and block them on Facebook. Obviously this doesn't apply if you are co-parenting some humans you had together. Now that we've got that figured out, FOOD!

all about **eating**

If more of us valued food and cheer
and song above hoarded gold,
it would be a merrier world.

J. R. R. Tolkien

There's an emergency and you need supplies! The emergency isn't a tsunami or a glamorous San Francisco earthquake or a *Wizard of Oz* cyclone. It's a heartbreak. I wish Jewel, the 90's singer/songwriter sensation, were here right now because she looks like an angel! An everyday angel.
Jewel might say:

Well in case you failed to notice,
In case you failed to see,
This is my heart bleeding before you,
This is me down on my knees.

Just look at Jewel, in case you failed to notice. Her heart is bleeding, she is down on her knees. She doesn't need a fucking sandwich. Or does she? Maybe Jewel loves sandwiches. I read her memoir and this subject never came up, but it's possible. Maybe that would be just the thing. Goddess knows when she was living in her car in San Diego she could have really used that sandwich.

Whether you tend to eat your feelings (and your feelings are very hungry) or you tend to avoid eating all together, it's time to talk about food. All the bartenders of the world know that often people choose a liquid diet after a breakup. But heed this warning by the Indigo Girls:

I stopped by a bar at 3 am
To seek solace in a bottle or possibly a friend
I woke up with a headache like my head against a board

Twice as cloudy as I'd been the night before
I went in seeking clarity.

It's hard to find clarity in a bottle. My mantra for not drinking is Feel Good Tomorrow. It applies to a lot of things.
Will I feel good tomorrow if I…
Eat that 12 am post-bar super wet burrito?
Sleep with that person I just met who looks slightly feral?
Drunk text my ex?

So what are your emergency supplies? Crackers and a can of tuna? My go-to breakup food used to be English crumpets. I toasted up those spongy little disks and slathered them with butter. And that was it. The problem I have with eating post breakup is crying. I can Kegel through the pain as good as the next guy, but crying and eating through the pain is another matter. Something about sitting down to eat just brings out the Niagara Falls of tears. If anyone among you knows my family, you know that (almost) nothing gets in the way of us eating. While we are eating one meal, the main topic of conversation is where will we eat next.

We took a vacation to Costa Rica one winter. My sisters and I went without our partners and my long-divorced parents were there, seeming for all the world like a couple. We spent our tropical days eating, eating, and eating. I can't remember one beach in Costa Rica. I do vividly recall a long table with heaping plates of gallo pinto and Lizano sauce. Are there other things to do in CR besides eat? Now you tell us.

If, even now as we speak, you are sitting on your sofa and wondering if the rock-hard piece of pepperoni pizza from three days ago is okay to eat, it's not. In fact, bring all six of those boxes down to the recycling bin. That can be your accomplishment for the day. For some of you, cooking makes you feel better. There's a cookbook you could check out called *The Heartbreak Recovery Kitchen*, by Jeanne and Lindsey Ambrose. I haven't read it because I have too many dietary restrictions, but please report back.

Food is life. Maybe it's time to subscribe to one of those healthy food delivery services. Which brings me to the cruelest part of a breakup. When a family experiences the birth of a baby, friends make them a casserole. But nobody bothers to make a meal train for the heartbroken.

Married people get wedding gifts of dinner sets, fine china, and travel money. Why do they need those things? They have a spouse! It's the newly single who need fine china to break against the kitchen wall.

My digestive problems led me to a nutritionist. In one of our sessions, she talked about body confidence. But it wasn't what I thought it would be. It wasn't about accepting your body just as it is (which I am, of course, all for); it was something deeper. She described body confidence as being confident that you can heal yourself. That you can know what to eat, what supplements or herbs to take, what foods to avoid to take care of yourself, to heal yourself. Body confidence can be a gift you finally give yourself after all this heartbreak crap.

Let's talk about taking yourself out to eat. It sends a message to yourself that you are good company, you're not going to miss out on life's experiences, and you are a hot date! I know some of you flat out refuse to eat out by yourself and I respect that. I find that as long as I have a journal, a book, a phone, a computer, a Real Doll, and a puppet, it's fine. But in all seriousness, eating by yourself can be done with dignity, by bringing your journal or a book. It's a powerful demonstration of self-love and acceptance to treat yourself to a nice meal. Another option is to eat at a sushi bar or restaurant bar so you can chat with the people next to you if you want.

Once you get past the host saying: "Just one?" while looking behind you for an imaginary date, it isn't so bad. Your server might not be your friend here, because what is a server if not someone who tries to coax you into overindulgence? *"Are we having dessert tonight..."*

- Write down four food items that will sustain you.
- If you are someone who wants to eat everything, have filling and healthy meals on hand.
- If you are someone who "can't chew" when heartbroken, try yogurt, soup, smoothies, and other drinkable items; but make sure you have enough proteins and fats to keep your brain working. You need your sustenance right now.
- Consider a healthy food delivery service.
- More help is on the way; at the end of the book are recipes under the chapter titled The Heart Healing Kitchen on page 183.

two occasions: **day and night**

I only think of you on two occasions.
That's day and night.

Deele

Day:
Let's cover the basics. What are your first thoughts when you wake up? Sometimes we have feelings of anxiety, intense sadness, or lethargy. Mornings are rough because if we got any sleep it was often a break from the reality of our situation. Waking up brings that back into sharp focus. Mr. Gloomy Pants is right there reminding you of your pain. Fuck that! I know it isn't that simple, but still. You could try saying this to your shitty feelings some mornings: "Hey, I just woke up, heartache, beat it!"
If that doesn't work, I suggest the following.

- Do not pass go, do not think, just get right into a warm, wonderful shower. Water is the great healer. Showers are great places to scream and cry—bonus!
- Put on some super happy songs. Show tunes! Like "Good Morning!" from "Singin' in the Rain." "Happy" by Pharrell Williams is also excellent. Play them while you get dressed, eat, cry, etc. I suggest dancing around to them. Fake it until you make it.
- Go right to the gym, yoga shala, or beach. Don't think, just get yourself there.
- If you can get right up and meditate, sweet. It's a great way to say "hi" to your inner world as long as there isn't a war going on in there that you can't dismiss right now. I suggest a guided meditation so your mind has something to follow.

Night:
You probably had some night time rituals with you-know-who. Nighttime is couple cuddle time. So let's remove the dread from night and put some joy back in. We'll go into this in more depth in the Chapter "Night Moves" but for now just...

- Have a list of good movies to watch, TV shows, or podcasts to listen to (There are lists at the back of the book).
- Try Yoga Nidra. It's so good! You can find it on YouTube. These are very specific guided meditations that can take you up and away. Yoga Nidra wasn't originally for sleep but for a deep relaxation state. There are now ones specifically designed for sleep.
- Your nighttime mantra: Listen to me on this one. This is the only thing I am going to INSIST you do. It's that IMPORTANT. Do it even if you think it's hokey, won't work, is too new-agey. Do it. Just because I said so. And see what happens. Lie down in bed and put one hand on your heart and one on your belly and say inside your head, "I love myself unconditionally. I accept myself completely. I am whole, I am perfect, I am complete." Your mind and thoughts are all over the place. Let them land here. Say it 3 to 20 times. I am not kidding. I want you to do this EVERY SINGLE NIGHT. You can do it throughout the day as well.

breakup math

I'm still distraught over a seventh grade breakup and refuse to attend parties I know my ex will be at. At this point, my heartbreak has lasted twenty-four times as long as our relationship.

Lena Dunham

The usual math that is circulated goes as follows: it takes half as long as the relationship to get over a breakup. In my research I could not uncover any evidence of where this theory came from, just that it was perpetuated on *How I Met Your Mother.* So it's almost an urban legend.

A one-year relationship gives you six months to grieve. Like most linear assessments of the nuances of feelings, this is kind of hogwash. Also, if someone has been married for twenty years, telling them they will be grieving for ten is like a death sentence. I guess it depends on how you define grief, recovery, and recovered. Every once in a while, I will be caught in a moment of sadness about an ex from twenty years ago and it feels like a fresh wound. One friend says: "Usually takes me two years no matter what."

Perhaps it's nice to have something to navigate the chaos of the great unknown that your future just became. Sometimes it takes me years to fully recover from relationships that only spanned a season or two. As Veronica A. Shoffstall's beautiful poem states:

But you learn, with every goodbye, you learn.

While people have long debated the length of the recovery period, a new study published in the *Journal of Positive Psychology* found that most people are able to bounce back from a split in three months. Researchers Gary Lewandowski and Nicole Bizzoco questioned 155 people who had been involved in a breakup in the past six months, and found that people started to feel better and develop "strong coping strategies" at around the 11-week point. There are so many factors here, such as: Was it a harsh breakup or mutual? Were there betrayals, or did you grow apart?

There is feeling better, and there is feeling Better. Feeling better could mean you have resumed getting dressed, basic grooming, and occasionally leaving your home. It might mean you have some moods throughout the day that could be categorized as good.

coming off the **love drug**

I'm in the stage of the breakup where
I wake up every day wondering
if I should do yoga or heroin.

Kate Willett

Even if it all went south a long time ago, you were probably still getting some good love drugs, maybe just someone to spoon at night. So maybe this doesn't apply to you. But often, the withdrawal is simply from not having someone to constantly text with about mundane things. Post breakup, sometimes my friends and I will text each other more frequently and start the daily texts with "Good morning, sexy" or "Sweet dreams, gorgeous."

There is a face missing in your life. You used to see that face all the time in the kitchen, in bed next to you, and across the dinner table. Where did that face go and all the dreams you had together!? Argg! Don't start texting that face. It won't bring them back. Put them in your phone as Do Not Respond right now, if you haven't already. If you have impulse control issues, take them out of your phone and block them.

Just look at your own face in the mirror with as much love as you can muster. Make friends. Be nice. Remember that no one sees all the things on your face that you are most critical of, except that dolphin tattoo. We all wish you hadn't done that. But you were young! And drunk.

As for the missing dopamine and all, it could be a good time to visit your doctor, or better yet, your local healthy pharmacy, and see if you can get some natural remedies to boost your mood. I recommend St. John's Wort and Skullcap. Ask your doctor first, but don't get them so riled up that they're trying to prescribe antidepressants. This country is over-medicated and doctors are too quick to prescribe a pill instead of letting people feel a feeling. Do all the feeling you can and only resort to the anti-Ds if you really need them. If there's a black hole you can't climb out of yourself, then by all means, talk to your doctor about the Anti-Ds. Remember that if it's just the breakup getting you down, then your depression or depressive thoughts are circumstantial and will fade with time.

Sex After Ex

THE BEST WAY TO GET OVER SOMEBODY IS TO GET UNDER SOMEBODY ELSE

If a text says: 'Let's just be friends,'
It should say: 'P.S. I'm broken inside.'

Cathy de la Cruz

Conventional wisdom (and by that I mean almost nothing) says the best way to get over somebody is to get under somebody else. Is it? You want it to be true, don't you? I do! You want to say you read it in a book somewhere as you are trolling Tinder, Ok Cupid, and your local dive bar for some strange tail. Having rebound sex, casual sex, or any kind of post-breakup sex is like a potluck in Kentucky. You never know what you're going to get. In other words, there might not be kale.

In the past, casual sex has gone very wrong for me. While in the act, I constantly compare this person to my ex. Comparing their body, their scent, their night moves, their way of holding and touching me. In the still moments after sex, I get very pensive. I notice sex loses a dimension when it doesn't have love. This is highlighted because it was not so long ago that I had both love and sex together. It sometimes makes me feel more alone and I miss my ex more than ever before. Why is this transient person in my bed, I ask, where did love go? Where did my actual partner go?

Sometimes I get so lonely and longing for attention that I search Tinder. My presence seems harsh on this platform; I'm always rejecting people. And then when there are no new matches, it shows me that screen that says: "There's no one new around you," while beaming my image back at me. Is it trying to tell me something? Stop searching. Look at yourself; be with yourself.

A good middle ground between celibacy and shady hook-ups could be to start a flirtationship. Defined as smack in the middle between the friend zone and friends with benefits. It's an innocent little tête-à-tête between you and that hunky checker at your co-op, or a long-distance babe. You keep an ongoing flirtation while hanging out or texting or FaceTiming in the shower. It can include cuddles and kisses depending on your agreement. It boosts your bedraggled ego, and reminds you that you are still as hot as New York pizza. And like New York pizza, there's the potential to burn the skin off the roof of one's mouth. Just sayin'.

Then again, sex can bring all that good juju and mojo to the surface. Polyamorous couples call this "NRE", New Relationship Energy. It can give you a little skip in your step and something to fantasize about during lunch. It can get your mind off your ex and onto your sex.

A good middle ground between celibacy and shady hook-ups could be to start a flirtationship.

In her *Psychology Today* article, Susan Krauss Whitbourne, Ph.D., reviews a University of Missouri study by psychologists Lindsay Barber and Lynne Cooper (2014). "Barber and Cooper concluded that rebound sex serves a variety of functions for people who've experienced the involuntary ending of a relationship. Individuals on the rebound use sex to cope with feelings of distress, anger, insecurity, and self-doubt. They're particularly likely to do so when they expressed a strong commitment to the now-extinct relationship." In my opinion this leaves the rebound sex squarely in the category of a crapshoot. Is it going to help with insecurity and self-doubt or increase it? Whitbourne summed up the study by concluding: "Your chances of engaging in rebound sex are likely to be highest for a few weeks after a relationship's ending. If you're still seeking casual sex as a way to fill an emotional gap, it might be time for you to seek other, more adaptive ways to find relationship fulfillment."

On a weekend getaway to a part of Mendocino County called The Redneck Riviera, I stopped into a liquor store. I did something very odd. I am a healthy eater all the way. But for some reason I grabbed those terrible "orange flavored" Hostess cupcakes. Even before I reached the checkout counter I felt buyer's remorse. I set them down in front of the checker, who was a short, heavyset, older lady with a creased face. "I don't know why I'm buying this," I said. She looked into my soul from her deep-set eyes and said: "We all have to give into our cravings sometimes." Check in with your heart and see where it's at. Proceed, but proceed with caution.

put **your hands** on me

If you're anything like me, then poor you, you want to be touched all the time. You like hugging and kissing and snuggling and shagging. You're practically French. What's that you say? You are legit French? Bonjour! Mettez vos mains sur moi!

In childhood, every morning I jumped in bed and snuggled with my parents. One Thanksgiving, when I was in my early thirties, my dad credited these childhood morning snuggles with his marriage ending. I think his exact words were: "You ruined my marriage by snuggling into bed between me and mom every morning." Thanks, Dad. So it wasn't your unwillingness to be romantic, or avoiding feelings by non-stop pot smoking, or the fact that you… oh, who cares. I love my dad.

My parents always said: “Whoever your future partner is, they’re either going to love you for this or you will drive them mad.” Well, so far no one has ended up in the cuckoo’s nest.

So you can imagine things are kind of rough when my source of around-the-clock physical affection disappears. And yes, you guessed it, Physical Touch is my first love language. Have you read *The Five Love Languages* by Gary Chapman? Check it out sometime if you haven’t. Physical Touch could be your first love language too.

When I don’t have a main squeeze, one thing I do is heat up my heating pad in the microwave and sleep with it either across my belly or between my knees. I get massages, though not as many as I should because, like you, I am cheap about those things even though I was a massage therapist for 17 years and I know it’s worth every shekel.

One time I was so lonely and longing for any kind of touch that I let a small child I didn’t know rest her little dimpled hand on my leg on a Muni bus. Her mom didn’t notice. And it would have been rude of me to say: “Unhand me, you cad!” to a three-year-old girl. It made me long for a world where children really could trust all adults.

Some nights I so long to press my torso against a lover’s back that it feels like a physical ache. And then it passes.

Sometimes just a hug from a friend or even a stranger can get me through the day. In Northern California it’s not that hard to get strangers to hug you. I have hugged bartenders, enormous security guards, and people at feel-good workshops. If someone reaches out their paw to shake mine I often open up my arms and say “I’m a hugger,” giving them a split second to duck out of the embrace if they weren’t raised on a hippie commune.

- Get a heating pad and heat it up in your microwave before bed. Put it in there for a few minutes before you get in bed so there is already something warm and cozy in your bed.
- You can also get stuffed animals and a body pillow.
- Take a day or weekend massage course.
- Take an acro yoga class, where you do partner exercises.
- Do The Five Love Languages Quiz: www.5lovelanguages.com

Kelp from Your Friends

I GET BY WITH A LITTLE KELP FROM MY FRIENDS

I need backup, I need company
I need to be inspired.

Ani DiFranco

Do you have any single friends? Better yet, ones who are also going through a breakup? Good! It's time to reconnect with them. No, you say, all your damn friends are disgustingly, smugly, blatantly in long-term happy relationships? *How dare they?*

Some friends and family offer great support. Others, not so much. I have been my dad's daughter all my life and therefore I know he has NO SKILLS whatsoever in processing, responding to, and sharing emotions. But every once in a while, for shits and giggles, I try to make him enter this eerie landscape with me. Usually, when he asks how I am, I just say, good. But on this one occasion, I decided to be honest. This is how it went:

Dad: How are you, honey?
Me: I'm sad about my breakup with X.
Dad: So let's see, what have I been up to…
Me: Don't you want to respond to what I said?
Dad: About your breakup?

Me: No, Dad, about climate change! Yes, about my breakup.

Silence

Me: Google "What to say to your daughter when she's had a bad breakup."
Dad: You can Google that?
Me: Yes, you can Google everything.

Note: When I did finally Google this, there was information available, though it was totally gendered towards mothers comforting their daughters. Fathers comforting their female to male trans sons, and the other wide array of parents/child interactions, didn't pop up in any results. Humph!

Grab a good friend or family member and plan some regular fun excursions so you don't isolate and grow a beard and turn into a gnome who lives in a tree.

- Movies
- Bowling
- Taking a walk or hike in a new landscape
- Café Crawl: Start with decaf and then go from café to café increasing the caffeine until you have a nice buzz. Bring a book of poetry and read poems to each other at each café.

friday i'm in love

Monday you can fall apart
Tuesday Wednesday break my heart
Oh, Thursday doesn't even start
Friday I'm in love.

The Cure

A weekend looming before you with no one to make plans with can feel daunting. You were recently someone's implied plan. And now you don't have them to snuggle with on Saturday morning. To lie in their arms on Sunday while you scheme about a delivery service where sexy butlers bring you breakfast in bed on sterling silver English tea trays. Can't you smell those biscuits, that rich coffee, that bacon?! Then they come and take it away without a trace. Wouldn't it be loverly?

But instead, you are now waking up, safely yourself again, with no one in bed with you except your teddy bear and your 10 throw pillows. If you saw *Along Came Polly* you'll recall the scene where Polly Prince stabs Reuben Feffer's throw pillows. Pillow stabbing is probably sounding pretty good right now. You know what? GO FOR IT.

Friday night is date night for many people. Our shifts at the sex shop are done for the week, we clocked out of the cultish vegan restaurant we serve at, our drag queen wigs are all on their Styrofoam white heads waiting for Saturday night's big show. It's time to put the work week behind us. We can hire the twelve-year-old video addict next store to watch our children so we can go on a date. Except where did that date go? This whole thing hit me really hard after a breakup with my girlfriend of six years. We always spent Fridays together. In the middle of the night during one of those shaky post-breakup moments I got the blues real bad. I threw off my feather comforter and grabbed my computer. I sent my friends a group email with the title "Friday I'm in Love" letting them know about the special meaning of that night and asking them to reach out and make Friday night plans with me.

Billy Joel, my love and my life, sang: "Either way it's okay to wake up with yourself." I sing this little ditty some mornings despite the fact that Joel's wives started out about his age, then sort of daughter age, then sort of granddaughter age. And you start to wonder, did he really believe that, or does he believe it's better to wake up with a hot young babe? We'll never know.

I tend to plan an event or friend hangout per day for Friday, Saturday and Sunday. One Friday I was so desperate for an activity that when my friend invited me to a queer sex party I went simply because I didn't want to be alone. I entered a Victorian apartment with rooms designated for drinking, dancing, sex, and a dungeon for bondage play. If you must know, I remained clothed and untouched the entire night. I dressed in a blouse and slacks not unlike those the older Jewish ladies in my family were known to wear. My most scandalous moment was dancing on the pole that was kindly provided by the management. Eventually I attended a sex party where I was more of an active member but that is a tale for another book.

So what day of the week is the hardest for you? Maybe it's Monday. When I was doing tarot readings at a crystal shop in Santa Rosa, the owner wanted me to work Monday because she said Mondays were crisis days. The Lifetime Programming for Women nightmares that transpired over the weekend needed to be addressed on Monday by a solid oracle. Manic Monday. You don't want to end up with a week that looks like this:

Monday you can hold your head
Tuesday, Wednesday stay in bed
Or Thursday watch the walls instead

I want you to have loftier goals for your Monday than just "holding your head." Staying in bed Tuesday is acceptable and

Wednesday is fine, it's hump day. You've already gotten through two exhausting, heartbreaking days. But there's got to be more to Thursday than watching the walls. The yellow wallpaper! Quelle horreur!

Actually reading the lyrics to songs you have just been phonetically singing along to can be disappointing at times. I always thought the lyrics in The Cure's "Friday and I'm in Love" were: "such a gorgeous sight to see you eat in the middle of the night." I thought it was a subtle reference to oral sex! It really just says: "To see you in the middle of the night."

What ho? I'm the only one? Okay. Well, I had a friend who thought "Suicide Blonde" was "Soup and Salad Bar."

A few weekends ago, on the way to my belly dance class via Lyft, we picked up another rider. This beautiful and mysterious woman got in and asked if she could play a Scoundrel song through the driver's sound system. It had a great chorus:

Despite all the tears I've cried, I'm
having a good time, enjoying a
sexy weekend lately, all on my own.

It really spoke to me. Why had I spent so many weekends feeling lonely when I could be having a sexy weekend all on my own? I vowed to do a reframe. And in fact, my weekend was turning out to be sexy. I was going to belly dance class where I would undulate with a group of women, many of whom would be showing their midriffs. In the evening, I had two pieces in a Breast Art Show. Yeah, that's actually just what it sounds like. About eighty artists displaying their breast-themed art!

Don't just let the weekend wash over you. How about around Wednesday, when you are staying in bed, you send out some messages to friends and make some weekend plans. You can also check out event calendars in your area. A Friday night church group, a Meetup, a book club, perhaps. Try something different. San Francisco has a thriving kink community so there's always someone being spanked somewhere. If your small Mormon town doesn't have this, then maybe it's time for a trip to San Francisco!

When in doubt, call on your friends. My friends were just as sweet as pie to me after my breakup. They invited me over for dinner; they put out an array of crafts supplies: pens, crayons, papers, and glue; they projected Glamour Girls on their wall; they just generally made me feel better. If some of that weekend still finds you home wallowing and wall-staring, then at least journal about it.

Here are some writing prompts:

- It's great that I'm not with my ex because…
- I am grateful for…
- I am feeling…

And this:

Commit to sending an email or text to friends on Wednesday to line up weekend plans. Okay, tiger?

Who knows, you could come up with a song as gorgeous as "Friday I'm in Love." But no pressure, many factors had to collide for Robert Smith to be Robert Smith. He came from a musical family, he was raised Catholic, he married young and stayed married. Who would have guessed, all that angst?

let us go to the **dogs** tonight

If you must have a little bundle of unconditional love, just go get a dog already. Dogs in particular are shown to reduce anxiety, ease depression, and bring out your active playful side. Or get a snuggly cat. Or a hamster. Or a wombat. You can also borrow or foster one if you can't commit to being a full-time pet owner.

adult **aid**

Lots of people want to ride with you in the limo, but what you want is someone who will take the bus with you when the limo breaks down.

Oprah Winfrey

There's one golden rule that all parents adhere to: when you cross the road, you hold an adult's hand. It's not that you won't survive without it. It's not a rule that's never been broken; but it's a rule all the same. The idea being that the crossing is into the unknown and much could happen before you reach the other side. You can watch this ritual enacted at every crossing, that clasp of hands, that assurance that you are united. I just looked out my window and saw a two-year-old veering away from his dad's hand. The dad had to pick the boy up and carry him across. There are times in our adult lives when we could really use that hand.

Adult Aid is something some friends and I came up with to help each other do simple tasks that any adult "should" be able to do but often can't. Say you keep putting off making a dentist appointment. Like the last time you went, your mom was holding your hand. Maybe your sweetie even made those appointments for you.

This is what friends are for! Enlist a friend to sit on your lap while you make the call or have them make the call for you. My friend found herself in tears at Rainbow Grocery because she couldn't bag her own groceries as fast as they came flying down the conveyer belt.

Her wife had always done this for her. Veggies and crackers bumped into kale and yogurt. The people behind her looked on with impatient scorn. She burst into tears, admitting to the cashier, "I don't know how to do this. I just got divorced." The cashier helped her bag the groceries. Now whenever she goes to Rainbow Grocery, she asks in advance for help. Perhaps you can shop with a friend for a while, so as to avoid lonely-down-the-aisle syndrome.

It could be a good time to diversify your friend group. Perhaps bring in someone who likes to read and summarize things, friends who can make Excel spreadsheets, friends who are results-oriented, passionate, and mission-driven. Friends who are lawyers and personal coaches!

I wonder if I went too far in Adult Aid when I had my massage client reset my digital watch after I gave him a massage. Since spring forward I had been living in the past by one hour. He was dazed, but he got it all sorted out. As he exited, I said: "Hey, you don't have to do it again until fall!"

Adult Aid is often about someone just doing the darn thing for you. Maybe you need a friend to help you clear out the hoarder den that was once your bedroom. This is not a "trade," by the way. I am all about the barter economy. But Adult Aid is not that. It's not tit for tat. You just help your friend. You are never too old for Adult Aid and it can be available in times of joy as well as times of sorrow. It's a very loving act to help your friends this way or to let them help you.

Adult Aid is something some friends and I came up with to help each other do simple tasks that any adult "should" be able to do but often can't.

- Make a list of three nagging chores you can turn into fun friend accomplishments.

Feeling the Feelings

THE STAGES OF BREAKUP RECOVERY

After a breakup, my life is a lot like Pac-Man.
I spend most of my time eating and
being chased by ghosts.

Chad Opitz

I overheard a confident tween speaking of a knee scrape: "It hurts really bad in the beginning and then it gets better right away." If only heartache was the same.

Let us peer back into the source of the five stages of grief. Elizabeth Kübler-Ross penned them about coming to terms with dying. Let's hear directly from her:

"The five stages, denial, anger, bargaining, depression and acceptance are a part of the framework that makes up our learning to live with the one we lost. They are tools to help us frame and identify what we may be feeling. But they are not stops on some linear timeline in grief. Not everyone goes through all of them or in a prescribed order. Our hope is that with these stages comes the knowledge of grief's terrain, making us better equipped to cope with life and loss. At times, people in grief will often report more stages. Just remember your grief is an unique as you are."

In a *Psychology Today* article by Suzanne Lachmann, Pys.D, she adds relapse to the list and redirected hope as the final stage:

"As acceptance deepens, moving forward requires redirecting your feelings of hope—from the belief that you can single-handedly save a failing relationship to the possibility that you just might be okay without your ex."

I would add one more to this list and that's Absurd Fantasy. Some may see this under the category of bargaining but I think it deserves its own designation. Absurd Fantasy is imagining that your ex is going to show up with a bouquet of sumptuous red roses and a diamond engagement ring. That they are going to send you a lavender-scented letter delineating their folly and begging you to come back. That they will show up with a limo waiting to rush you off to a candlelit dinner in a restaurant where the city shimmers below and tell you that you are the love of their goddamn life and they can't live if living is without you. Or you might fantasize that they will stand under your window with a boom box playing "In Your Eyes." Actually I demanded that final one from a girlfriend once, as a grand gesture, and when she delivered, she held a tiny phone in her hand, so the impact was lost.

These fantasies are deadly in their own cunning way. I usually just let them run their course. Sometimes I imagine something else just as outrageous but not involving my ex. Maybe Ellen is cruising by in her limo and wants me to come eat lobster with her! Maybe I'll meet Gael Garcia Bernal and get all the vowels right in his name!

What are your stages of breakup grief?

Here are mine, more or less.

- Initial Stoicism: I'm so over you. I nothing you.
- Please can we just get back together (to make the hurt go away).
- Recounting all the things I hated about you.
- Recounting all the things I loved about you.
- Hopeless nostalgia, sentimentality, longing.
- Extreme self-care.

- Obsessive journaling, memoir writing, writing a book about breakups.
- It was all for the best.
- You're still tattooed on my heart, darn it.
- Absurd Fantasy
- The Geographic Cure
- Acceptance
- Perpetual nostalgia
- Safely myself again. Contentment. An understanding that it's okay to be in a relationship and it's okay to not. Rinse. Repeat.

What are your stages of breakup grief? Perhaps one of them is reading this book! Perhaps another is asking, "Are the stars just like us?" Let's see, according to Emma Stone: "I was crawling on the floor. I remember throwing up. I remember being on the floor…I have never felt anything quite like that. It was so visceral. It's like someone has killed you and you have to live through it and watch it happen. It was awful." Emma Stone's an actress so we allow for her flair for the dramatic. I never threw up, but I can relate to her other symptoms. You?

- Write a list of three to six stages of breakup and where you think you are.
- Or copy my list down and write your comments next to it.

no more i love yous

Oh, damn, you're in it. Aren't you? You are feeling weepy and lost and heartsick and heavy. Waking up with a ton of bricks on your chest; sleeping in a heavy quagmire of nightmares that leaves you groggy. It hurts, doesn't it? It hurts like brand new shoes, as Sade says. Wait, who was buying Sade shoes? Why, were they too small for her feet? It doesn't hurt like brand new shoes! It hurts much worse. It hurts like what's the point? Why get up? Why get out of bed? Life went from being in living color to being a gray scale. And not fifty shades of gray, just one sickening continuous gray. A gray rainbow.

And furthermore, where did love go? During the recovery period after a breakup, we often still feel tons of love for our ex. It's a river with no ocean to empty into. It swishes around in us, turning from despair, to anger, to sorrow, to hopelessness, to everything, and to nothing. There is a lover in us that beats their heart against the wall, saying, "How could it go away? The words were real, weren't they?" This can leave us searching our memory like a suspicious detective. Did she really mean it when she said she loved me? Or worse, did he ever really love ME or was it just some projection of himself?

During the recovery period after a breakup, we often still feel tons of love for our ex. It's a river with no ocean to empty into.

Love is real. And it was real. The reason(s) for it ending are also real. We must not negate the experience of it just because it has ended. It would be like saying summer is futile because it will eventually lead to fall, and for that matter, to winter. So much of life is just about the experience, and yet we want to hold onto things, we want them to be concrete and everlasting. We don't want to let go, but let go we must.

i **hate** you i **love** you

How is it that we are feeling a loss that brings us so much sadness, and then there are some days where we feel hot, white, impossible anger towards our ex? This teeter-totter from the watery softer emotions of love lost to the bitter anger can feel overwhelming. We can write ourselves off as cruel and irrational. If we are so sad and so in love, why are we having murderous thoughts of punishing our ex, of yelling at them, even belittling them by saying purposely cruel things? This is all going on in our minds, exhausting us and confusing us. These waves of varying emotions are part of processing this profound loss. We probably don't wish harm on our ex, we just can't think of another target for our arrows of disillusionment to strike. We are a punitive society and we want someone to blame. Even in the smallest matters, we look for the culprit. The crime of loss has been committed and someone must be punished. These feelings come and then they go.

building the **mystery**

Can you look out the window
Without your shadow getting in the way?

Sarah McLachlan

Building the mystery is a phenomenon that can happen when our ex cut things off abruptly and without a plausible explanation. This can leave us constantly battling between not wanting to be humiliated further by them and also being painfully curious about why it ended. Why? Why? Why? Why did it really end? But if seeing them is just opening us up to feeling our emotions met with a cold wall from the other, it is often better to simply cut our losses and sit with the lessons of letting go, instead of trying to know with certainty. Perhaps we can never know with certainty why a relationship has ended. Especially when many of the decisions people make are more about their life and not really about us at all.

It's wacky to think of all the ways we want to respond when someone breaks up abruptly. I usually waver between sending a Jim Carrey gif from *Dumb and Dumber:* "So you're sayin I have a chance!" Or my naked picture with the caption: "What you're missing." Or the perfect line of poetry. Or FUCK YOU! What are or were your immediate responses to the breakup that you held back or let rip?

back is **forward**

Think back on past times of heartache or change. We no longer feel sadness or loss after enough time has passed. Someday soon, this raw, bitter ache will also be a thing of the past. It helps to remember that with time, things will be resolved within us. What feels blinding now, will fade to gray and then black. After darkness you will step back into the light, and the joy you once felt will enter your life once again. You will again be able to celebrate being alive for its own sake.

will you **remember me?**

While we are doing all this soul searching, we wonder what our ex is going through and what they remember of us. We especially wonder when they have already started posting pictures of themselves on holiday in Maui with their new damn date. But even that doesn't mean they forgot us. That just means they met someone new. Or maybe it means their way of coping with the loss of us is to distract themselves with a new love and avoid feeling all the feelings. Perhaps their way of coping is to constantly post pictures of all the FUN they're having. It's their way of wailing, "I ain't missing you at all."

if only

We replay the scenes of the destruction of our relationship like master editors with tons of footage, to cut and splice into many different versions. We think back on what we could have done differently. We blame ourselves. If only I would have been nicer, if only I would have seduced her more, and on and on into madness and infinity. This is the part of us that wants control, the part that wants us to be protected from bad things happening to us. We want to throw our hands up and shake our fists and be given another chance. But the truth is, some things don't work out. And perhaps nothing we could have done differently would have changed it. In writing workshops, they say you have to let bad things happen to your character. This is how fiction, non-fiction, art, and human lives work. Bad things happen to good people.

In the book *Out of Africa,* the author leaves her beloved farm, friends, and community after the loss of her partner who used to take her flying out over the African landscape. As she leaves, she says, "Love your fate." *Love your fate.* It is yours. It is no one else's. It is unique, colorful, purposeful, and beautiful. Instead of shaking your fists at it, see about accepting it, and loving it. Maybe today just accept one part of it. And then more each day.

if i **cry** in your shower

So forgive me love if I cry in your shower
So forgive me love for salt in our bed
So forgive me love if I cry all afternoon

Alanis Morissette

Relish your sadness. It's the other side of when you fell in love. Love is at the root of it all. It reminds you that you are alive, intensely alive these days. It's a miracle that you can feel something so intensely. There are cultures that feel more at home with the poignancy of life, its moods, and its melancholies. I'd venture to name Japan, France, and Russia among them. The Russians say: "A day without misery is like a day without sunshine." This is, according to my Russian brother-in-law, a very common saying. Apparently in Russian it sounds very poetic and jovial. There are times after a breakup that I am frankly amazed at my ability to feel so much, to cry so hard, to long so desperately for what was, and what will never be again.

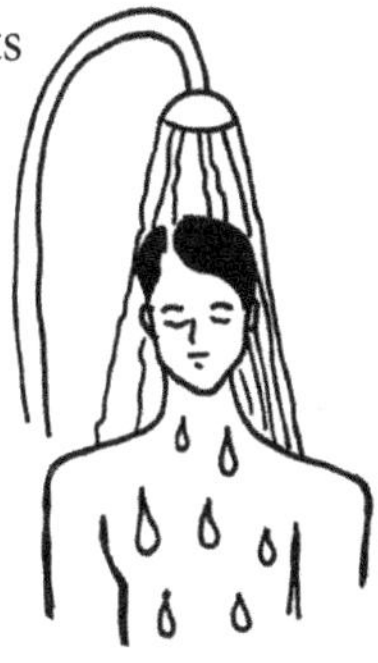

Two of my favorite places to cry are the shower (the psychic phone booth) and the car. I realize it's technically dangerous to cry in a car, but less dangerous than many other things I have done in cars. How much time and space can you make for this sadness? Grief circles are popping up here and there to help people feel less alone in their loneliness, sadness, and heartache.

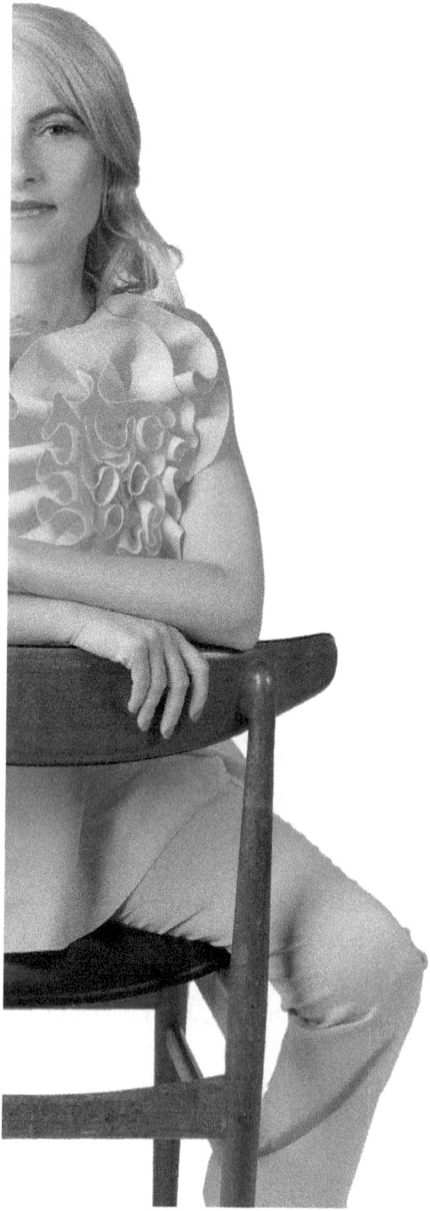

In The Middle

WHAT TO EXPECT WHEN YOU'RE STILL DESPAIRING

I never really understand the word 'loneliness.' As far as I was concerned, I was in an orgy with the sky and the ocean, and with nature.

Björk

Good, you're still reading! You are (hopefully) mostly alive. Functional enough to read is good enough for now. If you are reading this chronologically, then you just got some guidance on the issues that come up in the beginning of a breakup. If you want some extra support on letting go, try one of the breakup rituals in this section. My coaching clients have found it to be one of the most profound and effective parts of this process. Below you will find a quick list of pick-me-ups.

mood **kickstarters**

- **Roar**: Put "Roar" by Katy Perry and "Eye of the Tiger" by Survivor (or an upbeat "I'm awesome" song) on in a loop, and jog around the block three times, occasionally raising your fists in the air in triumph and air punching in front of you.
- **Laugh:** Watch standup comedy on YouTube, Netflix etc. I recommend Ellen, Tiffany Haddish, Trevor Noah, and Jen Kirkman. There is an explosion of stand-up right now, so there's a lot to laugh about.
- **Scrub**: Turn on the heater in your bathroom and dry brush your whole body. This will stimulate all the cells and bring vigor into your senses. Alternately, you can take a shower and use a soapy loofa. As you scrub, tell your body you are waking it up and bringing it aliveness.
- **Write:** Write a really, really bad poem (in your journal) and promise to never show it to ANYONE. In one week, show it to a friend.
- **Bad Date**: Go on bad Tinder dates (I said it). A bad date makes for a fun story. For example: "Lonely Republican woman looking for lesbian experience." Going on this date is more interesting than what you were planning to do with your night, just admit it. My friend once went on a date with a woman who brought her puppet along. She insisted he speak directly to her puppet instead of to her. Someone out there is definitely weirder than you.
- ***Sex and the City* Therapy:** Watch the scene in the *Sex and the City* movie where Carrie hits Big with flowers. Watch it as many times as needed. It's strangely curative.
  Search for: Sex and the City Carrie's Humiliated (2008)

the breakup ritual
a knife and five cranberries:

Make the first bottle you consume in this place a relic. Place it on whatever altar you fashion with a knife and five cranberries. Don't lose too much weight. Stupid girls are always trying to disappear as revenge.

Marty McConnell

Perhaps you did not grow up on a hippie commune with a guru, Hindu chanting, and hundreds of parents actively hallucinating while stoned out of their gourds. One day I'll tell you about the time my dad levitated! Stop laughing; my mom was a witness. Yes, she was stoned, your point?

I was ordained a Dianic Priestess (an all-female order of witches, thank you for asking) and have participated in countless rituals devoted to the moon, the change of the season, and so many more things. I'm Wiccan and I'm wild! And maybe you are fearful and intrigued by the ancient Goddess ways. Or maybe you want me to moon walk my voodoo talk right out the back door. Or maybe you come from hundreds of generations of great-grandmother witches, therefore my ritual rant is so last-three-lifetimes-ago.

One of the best ways I know to rinse that ex-lover right out of your aura is to do a little ritual. This can be what finally gives you CLOSURE. Enacting a physical ritual is powerful because you use your voice, body, and sacred objects so that it works on many levels at once. The childlike part of yourself gets to understand what's happening through a tactile experience.

Ritual can consecrate the end of the relationship. It can allow you to revel in its beauty, and let it go. An ending isn't a failure. That relationship was a moment in time that is now over. Like a sunset.

I know some of your eyes are starting to glaze over. Put your cell phones down. Stay with me. I'm about to go all *spiritual* on you.

Here are some options for simple and elaborate rituals:

1: Smudge yourself with sage. Get a bundle of sage from a health food store or crystal shop. Light it and let the smoke swirl all around you. You are cleansing yourself from this relationship and any lingering negativity. Many indigenous tribes use this technique to purify themselves or the spaces they inhabit from negativity and stagnancy.

2: Visualize a cord of light going from you to your ex. Now visualize cutting it with golden scissors. Their half of the "cord" returns to them. Your half returns to you.

3: Go to the ocean or a lake and strip naked. Run towards the water shouting all you are letting go of. Dunk. Come out. Well done, you!

4: Get some red yarn. Write on a piece of paper some things that you are letting go of from your ex, such as: "I am letting go of obsessing about you," or "I am letting go of anger." The list can be as long or as short as you like. Put the list in a jar and close the lid. Tie the red yarn around the jar and then around your waist. Say what you are letting go of as you cut the cord. Tie some of the yarn around your wrist or ankle as a reminder that you let go of this person. Discard the papers and the jar.

5: Photo Tearing. Make a paper copy of a photo of you and your ex. Or draw a stick figure drawing. Rip the photo in half as you say that you are letting this person go. Crumple up their photo, not in a harsh way, but do crumple it up. Keep the photo of you and see that you are still whole. Throw their picture away. Take the garbage out so it doesn't stay in your house.

6: Here's a more elaborate ritual: 10 Steps to Letting Go

Supplies:

- A small table or surface that is your altar
- An altar cloth
- Sage, Palo Santo, or Incense
- A candle
- A paper copy of a photo of you and your ex together
- Red yarn
- Scissors
- Four things to represent the four elements: earth, air, fire, and water; for example, a stone, a feather, the candle for fire, and a chalice of water.
- Eye of Newt (Just kidding but if you have some, text me your source)
- Optional: Cauldron, frying pan, or fireplace
- Piece of paper that has a list of all you are letting go of in this relationship.

Set the cloth on the altar and arrange all the objects on it in a pleasing fashion. Assess where East, South, West, and North are. Put each item in the appropriate area: east = air; south = fire; west = water; north = earth.

Light your sage or incense and let the smoke billow around you, clearing away the old energies and any remnants of your ex and purifying the space.

Raise the energy before invoking the circle. What does "raise the energy" mean? You have to turn on the stove before you fry anything, right? So that's what raising the energy means. Invoking just means bringing something into the space, like inviting a friend over. You can do this by drumming or chanting "Ma" or "Om." Say aloud or to yourself: "I am in sacred space." Stand up and face each of the four directions: east, south, west, and north. At each direction, say something like: "I welcome you, energies of the east." You can say: "I am in sacred space." Once you turn to all four directions you are in sacred space, between the worlds; what happens between the worlds can change your life.

 Take the paper copy of the photo of you and your ex and rip or cut it in half, saying out loud, "I am fully separating myself from this person. Our time as partners has ended and I am safely myself again." If it feels right, you can say things about the relationship that you loved. You can be thankful for all the details as you are clarifying that it has truly ended.

 Crumple up their picture (and any other paper things you want to burn and let go of) and put it in an envelope for later if you don't want to burn it. If you do want to, put it in your cauldron or in a fireproof bowl. Do this part outside so you don't set off the fire alarm. Burn the papers again, saying what you are letting go of. Note: You aren't doing them any harm by crumpling or burning this image of them. It's just a separation, the end of you being a couple. Have something ready to put out the fire.

 Next, tie the red yarn around your waist and tie the other end around a jar. Fill the jar with pieces of paper that say why you are letting this relationship go.

After a relationship has ended, there is often still "a cord of energy," almost like an invisible umbilical cord between you and your ex. You are now severing that. Pause and really feel this connection between you and your ex as represented by the jar. Say why you are letting this relationship go (like it was time, they were abusive, we grew apart). And then cut the yarn while you say you are permanently cutting the cord so that you two are no longer partners.

 Now, your portion can be turned into a bracelet or anklet that you wear. This is your *powerful* talisman. You can look at it every time you get sad, or obsess, or want to drunk text. You can touch it and say, "I did a ritual of letting go. That is in the past now. I am returning to the present." As Thich Nhat Hanh would say, "Present moment, wonderful moment." He got that right, along with pretty much everything else he has ever said.

 7 You wear this talisman until it falls off or until you cut it off; either action becomes the final part of the ritual.

 8 Light your candle, stating out loud what you are bringing in (like abundance, heart healing, happiness). It can be as specific as you like.

 9 To release the circle, face each of the four directions: north, then west, south, and back to east. At each direction say something like: "Thank you energies of the north, Go if you must, stay if you will, blessed be."

You can say: "The circle is open but unbroken. Blessed Be!"

 10 Now, about those crumpled papers or ashes. Either bury them in the sand on the beach, the dirt in your yard, or a park. Or if you want to be super urban about it, you can throw it in the trash. Just make sure you take out the trash right away.

If you start obsessing again, have a little talk with yourself: *That person isn't in my life any more and I am happy without them.*

Always Look on The Bright Side of Life

HERE'S WHY I'M BETTER WITHOUT YOU

Let's make a list of all the great things about breaking up with you-know-who. Here's mine:

- Don't have to pretend to be normal and functional because partner is not constantly witnessing my life.
- Can take up the whole bed. I still sleep on "my" side, but you go ahead and starfish it! Just don't end up like the *New Yorker* cartoon of an angry naked man curled up with covers only on his butt. A computer sits on the floor by the other side of the bed. The caption reads: "Quit hogging the sheets, loveless void!"
- Don't need to deal with someone's traumas from childhood as they blow up in my face during a fight. (I'm not bitter!)
- I don't have to feel bad if I don't like ANY of the movie or TV genres my partner liked. (My least favorite genre: any movie with all or mostly male cast and one woman wearing a dress and heels in every scene who is the "love interest," aka the "sex object.")
- Save money by not going on fancy dates.

- Save money by not paying for my partner all the time.
- Can do more morning exercise and yoga because I can't snuggle all day with partner (sigh).
- Have less urgency around shaving and waxing.
- See my friends more.
- Go to more orgies, sex parties, and swinger events!
- Finally go to Burning Man! Just kidding!
- Do that bucket list item they refused to join me in.
- Wear those clothes my partner wouldn't let me wear. (Uggs! Crocs! Pants that look like a lamb's fur!)
- Generally wear glasses more instead of contacts, dress more casually, and love myself just as much as when I'm all dolled up.
- Get all dolled up just to impress myself and delight others who see me sparkle by.

Write yours! Ready, set, go!

through a lens, **darkly**

It was as if my eyes had been traded for some other lenses, ones with a darker filter through which less light got through. I was fine with this. I wrapped my grief around me like a cloak.

Padma Lakshmi

If at all possible, try not to see everything through the lens of your breakup, through a lens, darkly. One time I said to my sister, while in the throes of breakup misery, "When I look back on the last decades, was I happy or was it a lot of false cheer?" What a dreary statement that was. From the lens of the break-up, I was always the one who didn't have a chair at the end of musical chairs. I was the one getting the mean reds but without Holly Golightly's glamorous wardrobe. I was the one who, when deprived of sun, got the winter blues so bad I called one of those suicide hotlines. The young man on the other end kept asking if I had a plan. "No, I have no plan, that's why I'm calling. If I had a plan, I wouldn't be, oh never mind." It took a lot to admit I was suicidal to you just now. But let's demystify it. Many of us have felt this way at one time or another.

Just because I got a dud on the hotline doesn't mean you will. So if it gets that bad, by all means, call the hotline! Here's the number: 1-800-273-8255.

Suicide is such a taboo subject in our culture, but I think many people contemplate it at some point in their life. I'm making light of it now, but at that moment in my life, I was in a really dark place. It's good to know there's a number you can call and not worry about the embarrassment you would feel when telling your loved ones about it. We are so afraid of burdening them that we isolate ourselves further. Do call the number; it will help.

Even my dud guy helped. I am still here! And always remember that family would rather have you be alive and crying all over them, than, well, you know.

Breakup brings us to the heart of darkness for so many reasons. We feel betrayed, deserted, rejected, and unlovable, to name but a few. This perspective will not be yours forever. When I was feeling the blues, one of my friends reminded me that my sadness was circumstantial and it would have a beginning, middle, and end. This is not a time for a life review or for making major future plans. Not until you are out of the brackish water and back into the bright turquoise sea of possibilities.

night **moves**

Perhaps all the dragons in our lives are princesses who are only waiting to see us act, just once, with beauty and courage. Perhaps everything that frightens us is, in its deepest essence, something helpless that wants our love.

Rainer Maria Rilke

When you are tucked in bed, presumably to finally get a break from your own brain, the fears, aches, and sadness comes rushing in. As if someone's just cued both Garfunkle and Simon and: "Hello, darkness my old friend," whispers into your ears. How can we possibly make friends with Darkness when he has brought his entourage of bullies ready to criticize everything about us? We need to prepare for the night. Have your happy basket ready and emergency numbers nearby in case you get too sad to be on your own. This may even be the time to try some natural, non-addictive sleep remedies. I like "Tranquil Sleep" by a company called Stress Relax. It features Melatonin, 5-HTP, and Suntheanine. Ask your doctor first. They come in these almost-too-delicious chewable pills.

Think about how babies are put to bed. They have rituals. They are fed and bathed, and lights are turned out. You could start a nightly bath routine or shower using only candlelight. Dim the lights an hour before bed and try putting away your devices then, too.

- Create a new night routine such as yoga stretches (can be done in bed), reading, lighting candles in your room, or bathing.
- Write what you are grateful for in your journal.

Eventually the night and darkness will be your friends again.

that **spring** in your step!

Spring is nature's way of saying: Let's party!

Robin Williams

Recovery from a breakup looks like spring feels. We are renewed, there are daffodils bursting out of our chests, we finally feel good again just because. I can survive a breakup much better in spring than in winter. So if someone is going to date and then break up with me, I prefer we get through the holidays and Valentine's Day. Anything after the Spring Equinox is fine. Well, it's not fine, but it will do.

So how can we feel a little spring even in midwinter or the Winter of our Discontent that is playing itself out like a Tennyson play in our very soul? Well, see the *Geographic Cure* chapter and get thee on a plane to warmer climates! Spring is about rebirth and renewal and you have experienced a death of sorts. The death of the dream that was US. Maybe you can see, even now from your tower of tissues, some vague outline of the goodness that is right around the corner.

pronoia

For starters, be open to new experiences, trust your gut wisdom, expect good fortune, see the bright side of challenging events, and master the art of maximizing serendipitous opportunities.

Rob Brezsney

The astrologer Rob Brezsny introduced me to the term pronoia. It's the opposite of the plague of paranoia that has infected our lands. Brezsny has a book about it called *Pronoia is the Antidote for Paranoia: How the Whole World is Conspiring to Shower You with Blessings*. What if that was your default assumption about the world? When you're spacing out, or daydreaming, or waiting in line, what if your mind had this buzz in the background that said even now all of humanity and the universe are sending me luck, good juju, blessings, candy, wealth, happiness? Not bad, right? Brezsny's book is chock full of ideas and exercises that will rearrange your brain into a more joyous repository for good thoughts.

There is a fine herstory of pronoia in literature. J.D. Salinger alludes to pronoia via his character Seymour Glass in *Raise High the Roof Beam, Carpenters.* Glass writes in his diary: "Oh, God, if I'm anything by a clinical name, I'm a kind of paranoiac in reverse. I suspect people of plotting to make me happy." Plotting to make him happy? We could all take a page out of Glass's diary!

The Alchemist by Paulo Coelho is imbued throughout with pronoia philosophy. It would be a lovely read for you right now. No need to jot it down; it's in your reading list at the end of this book, as is *Pronoia.*

In *The Alchemist,* the protagonist is a young shepherd who learns from an old king about having a Personal Legend. "Your Personal Legend is what you have always wanted to accomplish. Everyone, when they are young, knows what their Personal Legend is." He also says: "When you want something, all the universe conspires in helping you to achieve it." Even if what you are trying to achieve right now is to get out of bed before noon, or sustain a good mood for five minutes, this is great manna for your recovering soul.

In this very moment, pause and picture all those chubby glitter-covered angels bopping about, working day and night to make things awesome for you! They speak twenty languages! They wear sequined boxer shorts! They have been waiting for you to notice them. They've been on the *Magical Mystery Tour* for decades with the Beatles and they are waiting to take you away. So shake off that paranoia that you are unlovable, that you won't find another mate, and that people are saying mean things about you. It's just not so. People are saying nice things about you behind your back. The *Magical Mystery Tour* is waiting to take you away, to take you away…

When you're spacing out, or day-dreaming, or waiting in line, what if your mind had this buzz in the background that said even now all of humanity and the universe are sending me luck, good juju, blessings, candy, wealth, happiness?

Get Out There!

BREAKFAST AT TIFFANY'S

The mean reds are horrible. Suddenly you're afraid and you don't know what you're afraid of. Do you ever get that feeling? ... Well, when I get it the only thing that does any good is to jump in a cab and go to Tiffany's. Calms me down right away. The quietness and the proud look of it. Nothing very bad could happen to you there.

George Axelrod

Where is your *Breakfast at Tiffany's* when you get the Mean Reds? A museum? A donut shop? That little park with the little bench where… oh yeah, where you and your ex used to... No, don't go there. If you haven't seen the movie, it's a CLASSIC. And I totally recommend watching it right now!

What would Holly Golightly do? She'd throw a party. Or at least she'd stare at jewelry by herself wearing a fucking fabulous outfit and sipping a latte. Why not take yourself on a similar lil' date this week? If you never do this, it's time, my darling. Being single definitely means enjoying your own damn company. Go on what Julia Cameron calls an artist date. For you, it's just an "I love myself so much" date. It can be taking yourself to the movies, or an art gallery, or one of those fat-positive feminist/intersectional vegan strip clubs that are popping up all over the country these days, especially in the south. Or just treat yourself to an ice cream cone. But while you do, whisper to yourself: *Hey, just so you know, self, I am doing this because I love you.*

movers **and** shakers

An exercise outfit helps because it sets this time apart from the rest of your day and makes it matter more.

Jane Fonda

People feel better about everything when they exercise. Duh. You already knew that. You were born knowing that. That's why you were the captain of the toddler football team. This is one thing science, psychology, Oprah, and literally *every* other source agrees on. All I can add to the conversation is to encourage you to find something you enjoy doing. If you reach for your anxiety meds when someone ominously mentions "the outdoors" then get your fine booty into the gym. If gyms make you cringe (all that metal, all those meatheads) then don't gym.

Walking is a great way to shift perspective and get out of your head and into the world. Even if you are still in your head, the smells, sights, and scenery of the outdoors are going to open you up. Maybe you just get that warm smile from a complete stranger that is so fabulous, its essence stays with you all day. Once I was walking by myself near Dolores Park in San Francisco as a tall woman glided towards me. She had a hoodie that obscured her face. Just as we passed each other, we both looked up and smiled both openly and flirtatiously. It was such a moment! All on its own. I wondered if I should have run after her and gotten her number, but it was such a precious moment that I think that was all it was meant to be.

Julia Cameron writes, in her book *Walking in this World*: "We live as we move, a step at a time, and there is something in gentle walking that reminds me of how I must live if I am to savor this life that I have been given."

Or you could dance or skip or volunteer for something strenuous. You know how your grandpa always said: "When I was a kid, we didn't go to the gym. Our lives were strenuous. We carried bricks. We built things." My grandpas never said that, but you get the idea.

If you haven't been a mover and a shaker lately, how about this week you set a goal of just doing fifteen minutes of exercise? Sometimes I like to call exercise "feeling good moving your body." It's a mouthful but it doesn't evoke the satanic exercise crazes from the 1980s onward. Look at your schedule and see where you can fit 15 minutes in. Then go from there. Another thing you can try that has worked for me is to do just three cat-cows a day. Know that one? You are on all fours and you arch your head and rump up, and then you arch your middle up like a Halloween cat. I often do more stretches like downward dog and twists. It tricks me into doing more because all that is required is three. I have done this every day for over ten years! It's my little promise to myself. It takes about five seconds. Try this. It becomes a commitment you have to yourself.

Put on "I'm Feelin' Good" (Nina Simone version) in the kitchen and do the most dramatic burlesque improv dance you can think of while kimchee's fermenting and your mung beans are simmering.

It's a new dawn, it's a new day, it's a new life...

Another daily habit I would love for you to adopt is an ABS workout. Wait, don't throw the book across the room. Or at your cat! It's not what you think. "It's not what you think" is a great phrase isn't it? That's what I say when a roommate comes into the kitchen and sees me examining their food hungrily.

ABS is actually

Always
Be
Stretching.

That's right, I don't give a hoot whether you have abs of steel or abs of steel-cut oatmeal. Always Be Stretching can be life-changing. Have you noticed that some older people tend to atrophy? They get in their favorite chair, eat with abandon and seem to not really live in their bodies anymore? Let's not do that. And as for you women, no falling down and breaking your hips! If you stretch and take your calcium, this is less likely to happen. Our joints need lubrication.

I have a theory that when we stretch our bodies we also stretch ourselves out of old modes of being. We get ourselves out of being stuck in our ways and our mindsets by letting the life force flow through us via stretching. I can't be bothered to ask Science about this, but I know it's true!

You can stretch any time, anywhere. While waiting for something to cook in the kitchen, I do some squats. Even sitting on the John or the Jane or my gender non-conforming toilet, I do some shoulder rolls or clasp my hands together behind my back. I don't always limit this to stretching. I have been known to break into a full dance routine while walking down the street. I practiced some belly dance moves at Ocean Beach one time. Then I heard applause! Some person by the dunes had caught me in the act. Why do I break into dance? Well, because I want my life to be a musical. Doesn't everybody? Come on, a little bit, you do. Anywho, ABS, baby, ABS. Always Be Stretching.

You may need someone or something to hold you accountable to your lofty movement goals, so taking a class, hiring a trainer, signing up for a marathon, or having an exercise buddy are highly suggested.

You can bring a lot to the mat in a yoga class. I know I am not the only one who has discreetly wept during the process, and not just in Savasana. When I was in the getting-over-it stage, I went to one of those yoga classes where the teacher asks the students what they want to work on.

"Hip openers," said one student; "shoulder stands," said another; "emotional stability," I heard myself saying. Most of the students tuned out my request but the teacher smiled knowingly at me.

Is there a Vogueing class in your neighborhood? Vogue dancers tend to really build community while strutting their stuff. If you can afford it, you could join a trendy exercise cult like CrossFit. Or join the masturbation Olympics! Bonus if it's May, which is Masturbation Month! Now gingerly remove the two cats from your chest. Shove the dog off your thigh. Get 'em, tiger!

- Do three cat-cows a day. Get on all fours and arch your head and rump up as you inhale, and then arch your middle up like a Halloween cat as you exhale. Alternate. I would love to know that everyone in the Temple of Healing was doing these. Please join us and "the world will be as one."
- ABS—Always Be Stretching throughout your day and night.
- Take a walk on a street you don't usually go on this week. Start with just a 15-minute walk.
- Join a workout group or gym.

give back

Giving back is volunteering that gets you out of your own thoughts and onto the "helping high" of taking care of others. You don't have to personally nurse stray puppies and kittens back to life. Just Google some local volunteer opportunities. It could be tutoring kids, delivering meals, or picking up boas, fans, and lace between the acts at a drag queen show. Or picking up discarded thongs, gloves, and fishnets at a burlesque show. Did you know Madonna's brother used to be her dresser backstage? He had to pick up her discarded thongs!

the geographic **cure**

Tell your heart that the fear of suffering is worse than the suffering itself. And that no heart has ever suffered when it goes in search of its dreams.

Paolo Coelho, *The Alchemist*

"What's the geographic cure?" you ask in a stage whisper right before we board the plane to Zambia. The Geographic Cure is where you go far, far away from all that is familiar, from the flat that you shared with you-know-who, from your country, from your routine. In the Geographic Cure, you go up, up and away in an airtight flying device until you are anywhere but here. You can also be all-American about it and caravan across the US. Or join an all-female motorcycle gang. But I prefer to fly away from America into the arms of the world. My breakup herstory could be traced on a map with a pin stuck in for every time my heart was broken. The pins would go from Bali, to Spain, to Turkey, to Costa Rica, back to Bali (it's the heart chakra of the world, guys). I tried to go to Mexico in honor of my most recent rompre (that's French so don't ask me to read that word at a book signing), but my travel buddy cancelled the trip at the last minute. Maybe my Geographic Cure days are over, or better yet, maybe my breakup days are over.

The Geographic Cure (GC) allows you to get some culture and/or sun and beach time and just be. You get to be away from the normal circumstances of your life. You discover new ways of thinking and doing things. You are there to get your groove back. Does it work? Yes and no. It works for all of the above reasons. It doesn't work because wherever you go, there you are. There you are with your intrusive thoughts, your obsessions, your broken heart, your bruised ego, and your hopelessness. And still there's a robust moon crowning the sky over the night ocean. There's a sunset so beautiful that you gaze at it instead of photographing it. Somewhere in the vast expanse of the sky, you are reminded that life is a wide-open adventure and there is so much more love to experience.

I think my best GC was to Costa Rica after my longest relationship ended. And it wasn't just that I got to see more of Costa Rica because I wasn't busy eating with my family. My ex kept saying I would come back a Woman Transformed. This drove me mad. Why was she weighing in on this, pointing out how much I needed to transform? I said I'd come back A Woman with a Tan. That seemed a more manageable goal. I wrote a ton during the trip. Some of that writing is in a memoir I'm working on. As I enjoyed the glorious ocean, weather, and food, I kept wanting to sign up for film classes at the community college, but kept putting it off. When I got home, I instead enrolled at a life coaching school and became certified in coaching. The aftermath of my GC ultimately gave me a new career and completely changed my life from the inside out.

But my second GC to Bali was much less successful. Maybe I bought the ticket too impulsively. I was packing up all the remains of my relationship into a little shoebox (you know, the letters, the mementos, the dried roses). With a tear-streaked face, I got off the floor, sat at my desk and booked the ticket to Bali. But I was very lonely in Bali. As lonely as the day is long. Everywhere I went, the Balinese asked: "How many persons?"

"Just one person," was my sad reply.

On Valentine's Day, I was by myself in the gorgeous paradisiac Gili Islands. Just one person. I G-chatted with one of my besties, and I wrote, "I think this was all a mistake."

She replied: "Maybe you needed a beautiful backdrop to heal." Maybe I did. Who knows? Maybe the cure is actually The Cure. As in listening to The Cure in a loop, teasing your hair up into a tower, painting your skin pale, and mumbling to yourself:

Looking so long at these pictures of you
But I never hold on to your heart
Looking so long for the words to be true
But always just breaking apart
My pictures of you.

Is one ever emotionally stable enough to listen to this song? When it comes on while I'm driving, I just start weeping on cue. There are six men credited with writing it. Maybe they were on a stag holiday to Baja and they just passed a bottle of mezcal around, weeping as only pale men can weep, and then this song just flew out of them. They were collectively doing the Geographic Cure! It was The Cure on tour looking for a cure. I see I've lost you.

Here's a bonus: If you can do your grief travel to Japan, go to Gunma Prefecture, in central Japan, and visit the Divorce Temple there. Mantokuji Temple has a long herstory of being a refuge for women who wanted to end an unhappy marriage. And get this, you write your aspirations on a piece of paper and flush it down the toilet. The toilet deity will take it from there!

The stamps on your passports won't always fill in the holes in your heart. But sometimes they will. So start dreaming and scheming about your sojourn. Apparently daydreaming about travel brings you extra joy in life. Go forth. Be Bold. Be Beautiful. Carry a large stick.

doing what comes **natur'lly**

I wish that life should not be cheap, but sacred. I wish the days to be as centuries, loaded, fragrant.

Ralph Waldo Emerson

Guess what? Nature is good for you. And science is backing this campaign. I love when science validates common sense.

According to a *Business Insider* article, nature improves vision and reduces the risk of early death. If you have children, quote that last statistic right when you are shooing them out of the house to go play: "Go out and play, otherwise, early death!" The article also said nature reduces inflammation. Did you notice everything is about inflammation these days? We've all been inflamed and no one told us! When I was a kid, being inflamed was just called childhood. That's why we loved sprinklers! We were inflamed!

Metaphors abound in nature. All we need to do is slow down and observe. Learn patience from the spider that weaves a silky web. In observing a redwood tree you learn that everything good in life can come to you if you hold still. You don't always have to chase.

When I was having a hot springs getaway in Calistoga, I took a solo hike overlooking the town and surrounding hills. I watched a bird flap its wings and then glide. We are always flapping, we humans. We forget to glide, and rest, and appreciate our accomplishments until we have to flap again. Recovering from a breakup is much more of a gliding time. You flapped yourself out with that relationship. Just glide a little, like a hawk in the wind.

Another great thing about nature is there are no screens. I know you want to take pictures of everything you see and let everyone know you were here. But as pretty as those pictures are, they're just a moment's flip through the viewer's brain. Why not take a screen-free journey into nature? Because you know if you look at your phone to take a photo, you will see you got a text and a work email and then you'll cruise Tinder, and then porn will pop up and…So try taking a media fast during your sojourn.

In *Big Magic*, Elizabeth Gilbert talks about our reciprocal relationship with nature. How it's a conversation between you and nature. She cites a biologist who asked her students if they loved nature. They all raised their hands. She asked them if they thought nature loved them. They all put their hands down. The reason nature loves us is because we *are* nature.

Nature puts us in awe of its majesty and that humbling is harmonizing. We land right in our center. During city walks, I turn my attention away from all the advertisements and look at the trees, little gardens, flower bushes, everything of the natural world.

Going to a summit is a great way to get out of myopic thinking and be reminded of the big picture. In the heights, you can see all the rich possibilities of the day unfolding. You can spot your limitless potential just beyond those hills, hugging the vast sky. At night, the great blue beyond reminds us of what a small dot the Earth is. Carl Sagan, the astronomer and author, said it best:

"Look again at that dot. That's here. That's home. That's us. On it everyone you love, everyone you know, everyone you ever heard of, every human being who ever was, lived out their lives… every young couple in love, every mother and father, hopeful child, inventor and explorer, every teacher of morals, every corrupt politician, every "superstar," every "supreme leader," every saint and sinner in the history of our species lived there—on a mote of dust suspended in a sunbeam…"

Fire Your Critic and Hire Stevie Nicks

YOUR INNER CRITIC SUCKS

Many years ago I spoke with my life coach on the phone while sitting on my favorite neighborhood café patio. What struck me from that session, as hummingbirds flew by and I sipped my chai, was her saying: "You are going to have to accept yourself."

I was so frustrated with this concept. How could she tell that I didn't accept myself? I didn't realize it was so obvious because, in so many ways, I had a good image of myself. But I questioned my career choices, my intelligence; I had an inner critic that was always criticizing my best efforts. I kept thinking, I just need to do this one thing and then I will feel good about myself. I was always one accomplishment away from accepting myself, and thus it was never going to happen.

About a month later, I sat in my therapist's office. It was on the third floor of a gorgeous Victorian building. Her office was adorned with red carnations. I gazed out behind her at the glass door that led to a patio.

She said, “You are going to have to accept yourself.” This again. “Well, how do I do that?” I said, exasperated. She said, “When you realize that there isn’t any other way.” I finally got it. I couldn’t put it off any longer, and neither can you. Through coaching I was finally able to dismantle my inner critic.

Give your inner critic a name. Not your dad or your mom or your mean art teacher who said you should stick to Algebra. Just some name. Mine is named Bijoux. I tell Bijoux to fuck off a lot. Once, while preparing for a belly dance show in Costa Rica, I was on a lovely deck lined with tropical flowers. I turned on my music and did some hip circles and Bijoux piped in saying: *You’re really out of practice. You’re not a very good dancer even after all these years.* I was so frustrated I went inside to collect myself. I told Bijoux to scram (in my head). I went back outside and rehearsed and did a lovely performance that night on bamboo floors in an outdoor studio in the luscious, tropical air. Once you identify and name this little twerp, you can stop thinking what it says is true. It is not the boss of you.

You don’t kill it. You just slowly assign it a new role in your life. But first, just notice the kind of mean things it is saying to you, like:

"You’re stupid."
"You’re not good enough."
"You need to be perfect."
"I know you got that promotion but you didn’t deserve it."

“So,” you say, “what you are telling me to do is talk to the voices in my head?” Well, yes. So that’s your assignment. Name that little gnome of destruction and it will stop destroying you. You can say the opposite of each cruel thing it says. When it says you are not good enough, counter with how amazing you are. You will swiftly be on your path to loving and accepting yourself on a whole other level. The inner critic will be talked about in further chapters because I believe it is so important I want to keep weaving it into your consciousness.

stevie nicks, the sun, and you

I've begun worshipping the sun for a number of reasons. First of all, unlike some other gods I could mention, I can see the sun. It's there for me every day. And the things it brings me are quite apparent all the time: heat, light, food, and a lovely day. There's no mystery, no one asks for money, I don't have to dress up, and there's no boring pageantry. And interestingly enough, I have found that the prayers I offer to the sun and the prayers I formerly offered to 'God' are all answered at about the same 50% rate.

George Carlin

You knew it was coming. All self-help books address it. Let's talk about your Higher Power, or your Deeper Power for the earthy pagans in the Temple of Healing. In life coaching, we call it your Higher Coach. If you want you can just skip this chapter, light some incense, and put on Jimmy Cliff's song *A Higher and a Deeper Love*, and dance around your living room. Careful, don't trip over that bong! Do people still use bongs? Another uplifting Cliff song is "Wonderful World, Beautiful People." I heart Jimmy Cliff so much.

Our Higher Coach (HC) is a way for us to tap into something deeper, higher, and all-around more expansive than our sometimes myopic view. As you can see from the George Carlin quote, it can be the sun.

I'm a comedy groupie the way some people are musician groupies. I've been a long-time George Carlin fan. I especially admire his *You Are All Diseased* show. Sadly, when I finally saw him live it was with a boyfriend who had become my ex-boyfriend. We decided to still make the trip to Reno, Nevada, together, which was a mistake. On the snowy ride up, my ex talked excitedly about his new girl and I seethed with jealousy even though I knew we weren't right for each other.

Being a lucky California girl, I wasn't prepared for Reno's sharp cold, gunmetal streets, and voluminous amounts of cigarette smoke. To get to our room, we had to walk past the hotel's gaming area, low-key depression-in-motion. Gambling to me represents the saddest edges of capitalism where winning and losing can make or break a person, their family, their fortune.

On this particular night, Carlin had lost the plot. All I can remember is his suggestion that instead of just organ donors there could be other donations. Like some dude somewhere would really appreciate a vagina donation. This was punching down at its most crude.

But anyhow he found his HC and we bless him for it. Author Michelle Tea's higher power is Stevie Nicks, what an excellent choice for too many reasons to include here. But to start with, Nicks has a poet in her heart named Sara.

It may not surprise you that my HC is the Goddess herself or herselves. There are so many Goddesses that sometimes I address her as Goddess and sometimes I address the particular Goddess I want to work with at the moment. Or if you must know, sometimes it's just the universe, but to me the universe is also Goddess (Google "Wiccan Celebrities," It's fascinating).

Goddess worship may seem like some new fangled feminist fantasy, with no actual herstory. However, any study of the past will show there were Goddess religions, celebrations, art, and figurines on every continent of the globe. It was connected to a more peaceful, communal time. If we believe the patriarchy always existed, and thus war is inevitable, then we bring that into our future, into our relationships and ourselves.

Once you are in contact or reconnected to your HC, you can connect when you are lonely, need to make a decision, or need a boost before a presentation. You can tap into your HC when you are feeling lost and forlorn and alone. You are not alone. You can tap into universal energy via your HC and the best part is, you don't need anyone or anything but yourself to do so. Your HC is that still small voice that, when you get quiet enough to listen, always has the answers for you.

Finding Your Stevie Nicks

A great time to connect with your HC is in the morning before all the stuff of your day starts.

Sit up in bed or on your tatami mat or on a chair. Close your eyes and take some deep breaths. Try imagining yourself as a tree whose roots reach into the earth, connecting you to all living things. Then imagine your trunk is the part of you that belongs to the community of all living things and we all belong to each other. Imagine that you belong everywhere you go and that everyone you see is kin. Then imagine your branches lifting into the cosmos where there is so much space, possibility, energy, magic.

Picture your HC. All the answers and comforts you need are right here in the moment during this little meditation. Take a few moments to say or write any insights that come to you.

See, that wasn't so hard. It's like the hokey pokey except you do it alone, and you don't move any of your limbs, or sing. Your HC is what it's all about. When you connect with this power, you tap into a universal source of energy. Hot damn! Bottle that and sell it in the French Quarter of New Orleans! Or just give it away.

So who is your HC? Write and tell me. I'm intrigued. You've piqued my interest and tickled my whiskers; tell me more…

your **wiseass** older self

What a wonderful life I've had!
I only wish I'd realized it sooner.

Sidonie Gabrielle Colette

Let's imagine you are going to make it to the third act of your life and become a grand, wise person. This ripened "you" doesn't give a raccoon's fart about what other people think. The lines around your eyes and mouth are like the circles on a redwood tree, gentle reminders of the life only you could live. Sometimes I like to visit with my Wiseass Older Self. She usually looks like a mix between my glamorous Grandmother Muriel and Gloria Steinem. Grandma Mumu, as we called her, wore satiny fitted dresses with flare skirts in the 1950s. Then in her older years, she favored beaded Designing Women gowns with shoulder pads. I see them occasionally in my local Goodwill on Haight Street. Should I buy one? Or three, for my sisters and me?

If Grandma Mumu was going casual, she wore velour track suits with stripes up the sides; the kind that only older Jewish grandparents and young hot black people wear. She made getting old look so classy. When I was a child I liked to play with her waddle and the chub under her arm. I hope this was affirming to her. Sometimes at night when I can't sleep I imagine her presence surrounding me. She thinks all the things I worry about are so petty. Carl Sagan would probably agree. Didn't you love that whopper of a quote by him?

The Wiseass Older Self (WOS) sees all the way to the end of the story and knows it all works out. Who is your wise older self? Have life's ups and downs and somersaults left you back on your feet or knee deep in horse poop? As Oriah Mountain Dreamer puts it: "I want to know if you have touched the center of your own sorrow, if you have been opened by life's betrayals or have become shriveled and closed from fear of further pain."

Your Wiseass Older Self has been there and done that. What if you started spending more time embracing this figure instead of fearing its arrival? What if you started having the contentment of communing with the part of you that knows everything is going to BE? So since it's going to BE anyway, why resist and fear it?

Here are three ways to visit your Wiseass Older Self.

1) Sit in a comfortable position and take some deep breaths. Imagine that this presence is sitting across from you. If you can't picture it, try visualizing Pat Morita as Mr. Miyagi, Gladys Knight, Betty White, or Oprah, because, as we all know, all roads lead to Oprah. Imagine your Wiseass Older Self is saying loving and reassuring things to you, such as: What seems like a big, difficult thing now will soon be behind you.

2) Compose a letter "written" by your Wiseass Older Self and addressed to you. Let your WOS assure you that you are going to achieve your dreams of finishing that book, getting that job, traveling to Morocco, or marrying a wonderful person. Or maybe your WOS is kind of tired of your crap and is telling

you to chill out and stop worrying because you are driving them fricken crazy. Have fun with it. You can't get it wrong. Another variation on this theme is to write a letter to your younger self. For inspiration you can watch *CBS This Morning "Note to Self"*. If Oprah's *Note to Self* doesn't make you tear up a little, then your heart is made of stone! Find it on Oprah Winfrey's "Note to Self" advice "Relax" on Youtube.

3) Add another dimension to Halloween. Some of you already honor your ancestors at this time. But if not, place some pictures of your deceased relatives around your house, light candles, and remember their place in your life. Your Wiseass Older Self can meet up with your actual ancestors, which is kind of rad. Whoever thought you could be peers with your Grammy or Grandpa?

In our obsession with turning back the clock, we lose the grace and wisdom of the third act of life. Jane Fonda has a compelling thought about this. She suggests we let go of the image that the human life span is a peak at midlife followed by a decline. Instead she offers the image of a staircase: "The upward ascension of the human spirit bringing us into wisdom, wholeness, and authenticity. Age not at all as pathology, age as potential."

but **everybody** loves you

Think lightly of yourself and deeply of the world.

Miyamoto Musashi

So you are worried about what other people think about you, huh, now that you divorced the hedge fund millionaire? Now that your boyfriend has a new boyfriend? Now that your younger girlfriend replaced you with an elderly librarian? Don't knock librarians! They're super hot and the very heart of decency and democracy. But still, I'm sorry that happened to you. Ouch. That's tough.

Just as people never really know what's going on in our inner world, we don't really know what is going on in theirs. The couples that seem to have it all together will split in a month and the ones that didn't have a snow cone's chance in hell are a heavenly long-lasting couple. My sister says: "You know how you know when you are going to spend the rest of your life with someone...? You spend the rest of your life with them."

We make so many assumptions about famous people even though they are often misquoted and their images are manipulated beyond recognition. I vaguely assumed Audrey Hepburn had a bit of a charmed life. After all, charm beams from her whole being. I didn't know she was in Holland for five years when it was occupied by the Nazis. She said: "It made me resilient and terribly appreciative for everything good that came afterward. I felt enormous respect for food, freedom, for good health and family—for human life."

So now you are going to worry about what the Joneses think? Or the Zhangs for that matter? Or what anyone thinks about you? I guess that makes you human. Of course you are going to think about it from time to time. But we can't control the thoughts of others, so why bother with them? Who cares! Most people don't have that much time to think about you as they are thinking about what you are thinking about them. So Who Cares? Add that to your mantra list.

Who Cares!

In my coaching school, one of the graduates thought that phrase itself was worth the whole training.

Castles Made of Sand

THE TOWER

Barn's burnt down. Now I can see the moon.

Mizuta Masahide

I sat down at my tarot table at Twisted Thistle Apothicaire on Haight Street, to pick a card about this book you are reading. I picked The Tower. At first, I was so startled, as it's a startling card. I wondered why I got such a destructive card about this healing book. But in the next second, I realized why it was chosen. The Tower is exactly what happens to you in a breakup. In the Thoth deck, The Tower card shows a tower tumbling with figures falling from it while, on the ground, a creature spews out fiery tongues. The scene was not what you had hoped for when you first fell in love. Perhaps you were picturing shacking up together in a Mexican palapa or a destination wedding or running a hostel in New Zealand.

Above this fiery scene is the third eye that is wide open. And your aperture is wide open now, too. All illusions have been torn away. I learned to be a Tarot reader from my mom, Magick, so I'll quote from her book, *Magick Tarot*: "...the safety zone that we have constructed to give a false sense of security has become our prison, and it's disintegrating before our eyes." Even if at one time your relationship was a true security, it has ceased to be thus, and you are staring at the pieces. In time you will find that beneath all the rubble, you are still standing. You are still you.

According to Pema Chödrön, "To be fully alive, fully human, and completely awake is to be continually thrown out of the nest. To live fully is to be always in no-man's-land, to experience each moment as completely new and fresh. To live is to be willing to die over and over again." Pema doesn't mince words and she doesn't suffer fools.

There is a basic component to a breakup and it's change. Things were trucking along and then they stopped. A dead stop. A stop like a tiny death that feels huge and overwhelming. One of the things we have to come to peace with is that our future has been forever altered. All the plans we made to live together are no longer relevant. Or the home we shared must now be dismantled. The kids we planned to have will be unborn. The children we have will now have two homes. The travels will not be taken together. We will never again go to our favorite restaurant, and then have sex in the cramped bathroom.

In fact, now we are facing a future without a partner, a teammate, or a Friday night date. We have been dropped off at the bus stop and it seems all our friends are speeding along to weekend getaways in convertibles with sunglasses and goddamn scarves over their hair!

But "every exit is an entry somewhere else." You are entering a whole new world of possibilities. If you already knew what was on the other side there would be no mystery. When we experience difficult change, we wish it could just be anything but THIS. But the very change that happened to you was the very

When we experience difficult change, we wish it could just be anything but THIS. But the very change that happened to you was the very change you were meant to learn and grow from.

change you were meant to learn and grow from. It's going to be better than you could have imagined.

So let's go back to that third eye that is open at the top of The Tower card. This whole experience is waking you up to visions of the possible. Just as the pieces are falling and shattering, so must a new form be born from all this change. It's going to be better than you could have imagined from your tower. It's time for Rapunzel to get a real dykey buzz cut. Whether she fell out of the tower or scaled down it in the night, she is fully awake and intact. And she doesn't need anyone to save her.

the **lost** house

In search of my mother's garden, I found my own.

Alice Walker

So we have talked about some sad subjects in these pages and I have done my level best to keep the tone light. I want to talk with you about the Lost House. The Lost House is the last place your parents/guardians were together and happy before the arguments, plate throwing, affairs, divorce. Did you even have this house? The Lost House may be the one good foster home, or grandma's place, or that van you lived in the first year of your marriage.

So why are we visiting this place that is for sure haunted with ghosts of nostalgia? This was a house where you had some sense of wholeness, of a family tree, of togetherness. Maybe it was just that one summer by the beach where your mom taught you how to roll joints and your other mom taught you how to paint your toenails. Do you feel ready to walk through? I am holding your hand as best I can.

But for reals here. When I visited my Lost House I found a flawed, beautiful family that loved each other as best they could. I found a fountain of tears.

This exercise might bring up emotions, so you may want to do it with a friend, sibling, coach, or therapist. On a piece of paper, draw anything that reminds you of this house. It can just be a square with a triangle on top. Or something specific may come out that you didn't expect. That truck your uncle gave you. That dress-up drawer where you could become your true self. Imagine walking through the rooms of this home. What do you see? What of your little self or past self can you retrieve? Write EVERYTHING down. Now write what the smell, colors, and feel of the place were.

Circle the things that stand out in your words and drawing.

This is the Lost House you are now retrieving by reviving your memory. These are clues along the path to what love was and now is to you. Now write down three sentences you would like to say to the you that lived in the Lost House. Send your love and affirmation to that self in your words. How can you bring some of these feelings and images of love into your life Now? If you are keeping a journal put this all in there.

the never not **broken goddess**

To be human is to be broken
and broken is its own kind of beautiful.

Robert M. Drake

Have you met Akhilandeshvari, The Never Not Broken Goddess? Well, let me introduce you to her. Instead of shaking her warm brown hand, give her a respectful Namaste with palms pressed together in front of your chest. This gesture means, "I bow to the divine in you."

This lesser-known Hindu Goddess gets her name because she is not striving for wholeness. She is willing to break things open to find the deeper truth. As yoga teacher Julie "JC" Peters says:

"Akhilanda derives her power from being broken: in flux, pulling herself apart, living in different, constant selves at the same time, from never becoming a whole that has limitations."

Perhaps this was what Leonard Cohen was getting at with his lines: "Ring the bells that still can ring, forget your perfect offering, there is a crack in everything, that's how the light gets in." After major life changes we feel broken into pieces and we judge ourselves for that. Some of the events of late have left you clutching your mala beads.

All the gems, and mirrors, and ribbons, and brocade of you are lying on the floor. But what a sumptuous mosaic you can make out of it. A new life. But wait. Akhilanda wouldn't tell you to fashion it all into a statue and then decide to be whole again. Remember, she is never not broken. That means that only in pieces do the fresh possibilities come through. Only in flux, only by being spun around by the crocodile she rides on do we get to be open and dizzy enough to remain in the eye of possibilities. We can learn from this badass warrior Goddess. We can be fierce and fearless and full and limitless and never not broken.

April Hirschman

Make copies of things that remind you of your ex: Photos, plane ticket stubs, concert tickets, letters you wrote each other. I know this is a little harder in the tech age. You can also print out emails and Facebook messages. Sit on your living room floor with this raw material spread out before you. And start cutting it all up into pieces just bigger than a stamp or in varying sizes. Mix them around on the floor. Let that sit for one day. That night, journal about how it felt to cut up all those memories. (But you made copies so you still have the originals if you choose!) The next day, paste them all to a poster board, or something sculptural from an art supply store in the shape of something meaningful to you (a deer, a heart, etc). Now you have a new image of all the broken parts. Journal about how it felt to destroy those pieces and put them back together in a new form.

Your Self-Love Nest

APHRODITE SAID SO

Beauty, thou wild fantastic ape who dost in every country change thy shape.

Abraham Cowley

In *The Laughter of Aphrodite*, Carol P. Christ talks about beauty and how it impacts our mood. When we feel depressed, beauty is the first thing that goes. When we feel the mean reds, the blues, or the breakup doldrums, our personal appearance and our home appearance start to deteriorate. Are there piles on piles of clothes around your room? Are your drawers and closets actually empty because their contents are overflowing like volcanoes? Is there a modern art installation in your kitchen composed of dishes? Have you been wearing the uniform of the depressed for months? Sweatpants, baggy t-shirt, sneakers, or any slip-on shoes you could find. Have you found the perfect shirt/sweater/legging combo that you can wear to bed and during the day? Well done! I really like to find this in winter even if I don't have the breakup blues.

In lieu of a hairstyle, have you found a certain fondness for an old baseball cap that covers your greasy mop? I understand. We've all been there. But we can't stay there! Beauty, in whatever way you define it, brings your life happiness, order, and comfort. When we beautify ourselves, it affects our inner state of being. You don't have to buy a new wardrobe and wear a ton of make-up.

Try putting some coconut oil on your skin after you shower. Running a brush or pick through your hair. Putting on your party shirt, the one with all different beer or hot sauce bottles on it. The one with the dogs playing cards and smoking cigars. That one! Or the other one that shows a little sideboob.

Simple acts of self-grooming are simple acts of self-love. As for the recent stint you've done in the hoarders club, how about inviting a friend over to face the volcano with you? See the chapter on Adult Aid. Or hire a cleaner! It could be the best whatever dollars you ever spent.

Turn cleaning into a witchy ritual. There are many pagan and hoodoo traditions that equate sweeping and tidying up with clearing out old stagnant spirits and bad juju. Put a little rosemary oil on the bristles of your broom before you sweep. While you're at it, light some sage in a shell and smudge your space. Smudging means walking around with the smoke wafting about. Make sure you smudge all the corners of your room and maybe your whole house. Smudge that person right out of your space. Then wash that person right out of your hair.

Aphrodite is waiting for you to join her on the soft fainting couch where she is being fanned and fed stuffed dates. She is looking over at the turquoise pool and the ritual baths where she will be bathed in milk and rose water. Join her, you super fox!

space **speaks**

I wake up earlier in the morning when I have new sponges. That counter doesn't even see it coming. [My ex-boyfriend] would never wring them out. We were in the kitchen once, and I picked up the sponge, and it was soapy and wet, and I was like, 'See? These are the kinds of things that make me think we are never going to work.'

Jennifer Lawrence

Do you have some outfits that still remind you of being with your ex every time you wear them? Maybe it's time to just let them go. Are there things you bought together that give you a T. S. Eliot-level melancholy every time you look at them? Sarah Ban Breathnach reminds us: "Sometimes clothes hang around season after season, phantoms waiting for some unforeseen occasion in the future that never comes."

Even if it's not spring, this can be the spring-cleaning of your relationship life. For a great guide that you may have already heard of, read *The Life Changing Magic of Tidying Up* by Marie Kondo. Several of my coaching clients mentioned this book to me, so I bought myself a copy. I followed the stages of transforming my house by picking up each and every item I owned and asking myself if it sparked joy. About a year later, my wardrobe felt old and shabby again. I was partly disappointed with my wardrobe for the same reason you are, too many items are of the brand Mossimo.

Recently, I posted on Facebook: "None of my clothes are sparking joy, help me Marie Kondo." The next day my friend invited me to go see Kondo at SFU! What? She lives in Japan! It's not like she rolls through every week. Synchronicity!

The glow of organization emanates from her every pore. Can you imagine a life without the chaos of well, you? Sorry, that was harsh. I know you're sensitive right now. But a life without the chaos of dirty dishes, clothes everywhere, and never being able to find your keys would be pretty sweet.

Kondo may be small in stature, but she is big in vision. She advised us to touch each item in our home and feel the response in our bodies. This is not a quick fix technique; there is some slow personal inquiry to be done here. An important part of the process is setting your intention for your life before you even start organizing. She also asked us to not think of it as purging, but to focus on what we were keeping, the truly cherished items.

If you think it's weird that she treats her socks as sort of sentient beings who desire to be folded in half instead of balled up, well then, I guess you have a case. But I think it's bold and shamanic that she anthropomorphizes everything. If you are looking for an expert on organization, wouldn't you choose a Japanese woman who comes from a country where the art of sushi, Joman Ceramics, Zen ink painting, and Kabuki all originate? It seems a wiser choice than an American who hails from a country where the term hoarder was surely coined? This careful taking stock of your belongings leads to peace of mind when you enter a beautiful room. Then your eyes can rest on a thriving plant or vase of flowers instead of Leaning Towers of your Pisa messes otherwise known as denial piles.

Inspired by Kondo, I want to add my own little clean-up advice that has been Life Changing for me. I tell myself that any clothes I don't put away directly after they come off my body are sabotaging my Future Self! Get it? That Future Self will have to deal with not one item but a whole room draped with clothes! And then you have to take all the time to clean up all those clothes.

Tip: When clothes come off your body, one of three things happens. They get:

- hung up
- folded up
- or thrown in the hamper.

If you do this, the world of organization is yours! Take good care of your Future Self. The only exception, of course, is if you are in the throes of passionate seduction. Then let the thongs fall where they may. Your future self won't mind picking up those items, wink wink.

A messy room is just a list of decisions unmade. You can do what my family calls a three-song cleanup. This could also be a fun time to get out your Feng Shui bagua and see what's happening in the different sections of your room. It's a simple map you superimpose over each room to see where relationship, fame (Fame!), abundance, career, etc, are. Perhaps you can pay special attention to the relationship corner. You could remove the dead fichus and those stacks of paper you've been avoiding. You can put in items that center on self-love or attracting a new mate. This could be a good time to toss the sheets out and treat yourself to a new set that is free of memories.

It's also time to do a thorough sweep of all the stuff your ex managed to burrow around the house. This can be quite painful, but necessary. And it can show up anywhere. At my mom's house, there was a toothbrush in the bathroom carefully labeled with my ex's name for when we visited. I sure wasn't happy to come across that. But each time I remove all the physical evidence of past heartache, it seems to bring lightness and hope cascading in rainbow glitter over the future.

- Put on three songs, and see how much cleaning you can get done in that amount of time. Sometimes this can trick you into doing more songs.
- Print out a bagua and apply it to your room. Make changes accordingly.

happy basket

I get the winter blues. Also known as SADD, seasonal depression, Where's the Fucking Sun Syndrome. (I know, I know, I live in California! But Northern California as in San Francisco—Fog City, baby). When these blues intersect with a breakup it's real bad. One winter, I just couldn't get out of my mood. Some friends suggested antidepressants. I went to see my doctor, but decided against it.

That night I left my house at 10:00 pm. I walked to the shadowy entrance of Golden Gate Park at Haight. This is not a safe place at night. In the day it's safe, but you might be sexually harassed and offered buds, green buds. I was so lost in my sadness I guess I just wanted to get lost in the park, in the darkness, surrounded by the wet grass, drooping trees, and murky pond that would have reflected the moon if only the moon was in sight. I had options. I could walk deeper into the park, into danger, into the unknown, putting myself at risk because I felt I had nothing left to lose. But my natural self-preservation instinct kicked in. I slowly walked out of the park and onto Haight Street. I got the usual round of "compliments" from the homeless population. And I got to thinking how there are no sleigh bell reindeer songs about seasonal depression or the breakup blues.

It could go something like:

We're depressed tonight
With insomnia in a winter underworld
In the alley we can build a snowman
And pretend that he is Jackson Browne
He'll say, are you married…
We'll say: "REALLY? Really, Jackson Browne snowman?
I am lying in the snow in a puddle of tears shaking and
repeating my ex's name and you are …Asking if I'm married?
I expected more from you, Jackson Browne. You're running on
empty alright!

Oh, I've lost the plot. My sister, seeing me in a bout of SADD, said I needed to make a Happy Basket.

The Happy Basket (or comfort drawer) is a little basket with all good mementos that make you feel happy. Hold up, I'm going to go grab mine, it's under my bed. Maybe I should put it somewhere more accessible, but San Francisco storage space is at a premium, as you can imagine.

Okay, so mine has the following:

- Sage in a shell all ready to clear the negative juju away.
- A pretty little flower candle I bought in Bali.
- A velvety pink pouch with lavender in it. Lavender is uplifting and soothing.
- A bag of organic chamomile tea.
- A Rumi quote: "What you seek is seeking you." Yeah, but "What the fuck is taking you so long?" you say.
- Some tissues to catch the tears.
- Another quote, this time on a sticker with a hummingbird getting nectar from a flower: "Faith is the bird that feels the light when the dawn is still dark."
- A bunch of cards of all stripes, like birthdays and thank-yous. Oh cards! They are blessed and more rare these days.
- An index card that says List of People to Call. I have 8 people on it; most of them are related to me, some are friends, and one is my life coach.

So you get the idea. This is a gift from your happier self to give to your less happy self. It's really cheery and a good antidote for those dark nights of the soul that come around from time to time.

Supplies:

- A medium basket
- Fun-filled photos
- Cards
- Your favorite tea bag
- A copy of your emergency phone numbers

Fill up a basket using suggestions from the above list and the one on the previous page.

Put the basket under or near your bed and bring it out as needed.

You are not alone because people are thinking of you.

Unusual and Usual Recovery Tips

JUST FLOAT

When feeling good is rare and pain has become a way of life, floatation offers a fully supportive environment where gravity is released from the body creating periods of freedom from suffering.

From the Float Matrix website

I officiated at the wedding of two sweet friends one windy day at Dolores Park. As a thank-you gift, they gave me a float in a floatation tank. What was once called sensory deprivation is now called floating. That was an excellent rebranding choice, as no one likes to be deprived. Sensory deprivation is the cruelest punishment. Just ask those held at Guantanamo Bay.

I let years go by without using the certificate because it never seemed like the right time to go to the Tenderloin District, a neighborhood notorious for drug-related crime, and float alone in a tank. But we do wild and crazy things in the name of breakup recovery, don't we?

When I finally called Float Matrix to make my appointment, I got a recorded message that said, "Welcome to Float Matrix, your center for getting centered." Your center for getting centered! It sounded like I was entering a futuristic sci-fi movie where a woman with a tight bun and a crisp English accent would be the mastermind behind a hygienic death camp.

An American physician named John C. Lily invented floatation. He began testing it in 1953. It had a big resurgence in the 1970s and is having another one now. Notable floaters include: Susan Sarandon, Kristen Wiig, Yoko Ono, the late John Lennon, Carl Luis, Elle McPherson, Jeff Bridges, Tim Ferris, and Steph Curry.

There are all kinds of claims about what floating can do for you, including improving brain function and helping insomnia, jet lag, and anxiety. The Float Matrix's brochure simply lists the following benefits: stress relief, back pain relief, and tranquility.

I called Float Matrix a second time and got a real person on the line. I told her I was looking for experiences to help me get over a breakup. "It would be better than the other option," she said. "Which is a bottle of vodka. No one has had a breakdown and come out crying. It's mostly just relaxing if you can get over the fact that it's dark." "It's dark?" I said in a sudden panic. I hadn't given much thought to the sense of sight being removed. When I pictured myself in the tank it was always with a little light. A night light perhaps. A candle? Something!

The pamphlet showed a beautiful woman's face and neck surrounded by rich blackness. She was most certainly not floating in total darkness or how would I know she was a beautiful woman? The light illuminated and contoured her blissful face. After the phone call, I had small panics about the darkness, the claustrophobia, the unknown. I almost cancelled it several times. But I didn't!

To prepare for my visit, Float Matrix suggested:

1. Eat a light meal 1.5 hours prior to floating.
2. Don't drink any caffeine up to 6 hours prior to floating.
3. If you wear contacts, be prepared to remove them.
4. Don't shave within 4 hours or wax within 24 hours prior to float.

In the elevator on the way to my appointment, an older woman got in right after me. "Oh, you're going down," she said while entering the elevator. I was, in fact, going to the basement.

"I'm going to float."

"I've never been down there. Well, good girl, get your float on!"

"Thanks, first time."

As I got out she said: "Maybe I'll see you again."

Maybe she would or maybe no one would ever see me again. Was I entering the Elysian Fields? Was this elevator lady the last human to see me alive?

Maybe this was a trap. Maybe Float Matrix led to some crazy underground tunnel. Maybe it was an organ thief scam! I exited to a series of long hallways lined with mirrors for no apparent reason.

It was the same lady I spoke to on the phone. She showed me to the simple bathroom made slightly elegant by sconces beaming diffused golden light. I showered and dried off with a rough towel and put on the slightly less rough robe. She showed me to a room sectioned off with curtains. Everything was quiet except for the buzz of something. No one else was in the basement with us.

"Is it weird being down here all day without windows?" I asked.

"No, I live in a basement apartment."

"Are you a Scorpio?"

"Yes."

Well, I was spot on about her sign! She showed me the earplugs and a little floaty cradle for my neck. Then I was left alone with a long gray rectangular pod. Entering was a crazy thing to do. Like entering the door in the floor (Jeff Bridges was in a movie with that same title—*The Door in The Floor.*) Who enters the door in the floor unless forced?

I wasn't worrying about being alone with my thoughts. I was more concerned with the tight quarters, the darkness, and the temperature of the water. The philosopher and mathematician Blaise Pascal said: "All of humanity's problems stem from man's inability to sit quietly in a room alone."

Many spiritual practices including Buddhism were perhaps created in part to address this. So should you choose to try a float, let it be an opportunity to be as friendly with yourself as possible. In a study conducted by Timothy Wilson, a social psychologist at the University of Virginia in Charlottesville, published in 2014, people who were left alone in a room for 15 minutes chose to electrically shock themselves instead of just sitting and doing nothing. 67% of men and 25% of women made this bizarre choice.

My pod sat there waiting for my naked body. I got in and was instantly surrounded by warm, plastic-tinged air. It was evocative of so many things, yet completely unique; Darryl Hannah in her mermaid tank, a CT scan, the dark dome of the Exploratorium, being in the womb.

After the first few moments, I adjusted to the strangeness of the dark, where it didn't really matter whether my eyes were open or closed. This is a darkness not found in the city. I also didn't need to hold up my body, as it was held up by 1,000 pounds of Epsom salts.

As I floated, I felt a calm mother/child love pouring over me. I understood that my mom had created me, and simultaneously, my arrival created something that both of us were in together. It was in the flow that went between us. I felt a faint tingle around my belly button, the place we once were one. Throughout my time I kept trying to consciously return to that womb feeling, but could not, though I was intrinsically cradled in its metaphor.

Then fears started to pour in. I was in the basement of a building on Hyde Street. I was hiding on Hyde. Was this a game of hide and seek? Like the ones my niece never tires of? Who would find me? Well, the attendant would. She would knock on my pod when my time was up.

What if there was an earthquake or a fire? What if there was a rapist? I was such an easy target, naked in the dark in this rectangular pod. Gradually the fears disappeared. I didn't feel claustrophobic because with the darkness I could be in a pool on the moon or just floating in space.

Different songs echoed through me like the Beatles' "All You Need is Love." The song starts out with six loves! Love Love Love... It's a perfect way to start a song because it already gave you all you desired, all you could hope for. Love in repetition, love in double triplicate, love as a matter-of-fact and tangible thing. It's easy...

Movie lines came to me, too. From *Cocoon*: "We won't get any older and we won't ever die."

Oddly, I never felt the sensation of water; I was weightless in an unknown substance between air and water. I only adjusted tiny parts of my body during the entire hour. Besides that, I kept completely still. Much more still than when I sleep and turn side to side in search of the perfect position.

It was timelessness. I didn't want to leave. No desire to flee. My thoughts and me were just fine. I did not want to shock myself to stay entertained, though that is an unfair comparison, as I was having so many pleasant sensations to keep me content.

Towards the end I had no limbs, only energy channels like we learned in Thai massage class, meridians. I was just meridians floating in vast weightless space that didn't feel like water or being wet. I knew I wouldn't fall asleep, but I was very close to sleep, on the edge of a liminal state. I was disappointed, but obedient, when the loud knocks came upon the pod. I showered and dressed. Out on the street, I felt like I had received a light pressure massage. This would be a great massage substitute for someone who doesn't want to be touched at all. And isn't afraid of water or darkness or small spaces. I liked it. I would do it again. I could see that doing this repeatedly would bring a great sense of peace. Maybe this is the time to give yourself permission to try something different, like floating in dark Epsom salt space.

As the Beatles sang: "Nothing you can do but you can learn how to be you in time. It's easy."

Look for an unusual healing modality such as floating, acupuncture, Korean Spa body scrub and the like, and see if it resonates with you.

and stay **obsessed**

You've got to get obsessed and stay obsessed.

John Irving

Yesterday, when I was in my early twenties, I was so obsessed with the above quote that I wrote it out in graceful lettering and put it on my bedroom wall. The things I was obsessed with and am obsessed with to this day are belly dancing, tarot, magic, and art. Of course, there are more I could list, but those cover vast territory. I invite you to get obsessed with something besides love, relationship, and your ex. If this is the only advice you take from this book, maybe it's enough. One friend said she became obsessed with learning French. That was her recovery strategy. This idea isn't right for everyone, but maybe it's right for you.

According to *The Personal MBA* author, Josh Kaufman, to go from "knowing nothing to being pretty good" it takes 20 hours or the equivalent of 45 minutes a day for a month. I hesitate to share this because this isn't really about you becoming pretty good or even an expert at something. But it's an irresistible fun fact, no?

This could be a great moment for you to return to an old obsession (collecting navel fluff, fork bending, soap carving, samurai sword balancing). Or jump in and take a swimming class, ballroom dance, or do a Miranda July-style stunt where you upload a dance routine every day. The sky's the limit and the sky is no limit at all. So go get obsessed! And stay that way.

- Free write in your journal to discover three things you used to be obsessed with.
- Is there one that you can revisit now?
- What is one thing you are already obsessed with that you can become a participant in instead of just a spectator?

the fever of **creation**

Only in the fever of creation could she recreate her own lost life.

Anaïs Nin

If it weren't for breakups, the art in the world would be reduced by half; that may be a conservative guess. Breakup art spans all genres and is sometimes disguised to obscure its source.

Now's the time to take that guitar class, painting workshop, filmmaking series, or to join that anarchist silk screening group. Or to dust off that craft box you keep in an attic you are too scared to enter. Throw a crafternoon party! If you aren't quite in the mood for a party, perhaps you could craft with a friend or two.

When I was visiting The Ace Hotel, a hipster haven in Palm Springs, California, I found myself chatting with a cabana boy. His skin was tan from being outside and his blue eyes reflected the blue of the big sky and shimmering pool. My sisters and I were on a sister vacation so we were all wearing matching cherry bikinis. He brought us our avocado toasts. He mentioned that earlier, a table of people had been making art on the patio. They said they needed heat lamps:

"We can't craft when we're cold," they complained. Hipsters! So if you're going to craft, do it inside with Grandma's knitted blankets on your lap, or on your heated patio.

The other day, as I was walking down Cole Street, the street that's been my home for over a decade, I found myself caught up in such a good mood. I saw neighbor kids who were now young adults, I saw the couple walking their two big black dogs, I looked up to see the apartment across from mine where I have been lucky enough to have my sister as a neighbor for years.

I caught myself in a moment where I grasped the totality of myself, my habits, my character, my arts, my particular thoughts and I just loved myself. Usually this happens when all my creative ideas are spinning at once and I feel such pride in being a creative person. It's such a relief from the self-doubt and criticism that becomes habitual. It's so peaceful and good. It makes the whole tango worthwhile after all. In any moment you could, as Chödrön says, "find yourself in the center of a sacred circle." So if you are one of those people who tells everyone, "I'm just not creative," this might be an opportunity to take a second look at that long-held belief.

This is a great time to open up the copy of Julia Cameron's *The Artist's Way* about creative recovery that your aunt gave you seven birthdays ago. Your aunt knows best. Julia will get you off your duff and creating your stuff. She has worked with people way more crotchety and reluctant than you. Also, she is an all-star quote hunter. Being a quote enthusiast myself, I admire her skill.

Create yourself back into life, for if there is one thing we are all here to do, it's create! When the hands are busy, the mind can't get into its painful mind chatter. Bob Dylan once said: "[S]He not busy being born is busy dying."

A great way to be born is to make things. That's actually one of the greatest things about dancing as a creative practice; if you are focusing on steps, your mind can't wander. You could also join those free form dance things called Open Floor, Five Rhythms, Ecstatic Dance, etc. They put on soulful music and everyone free-dances about. Though be warned that almost everyone will be white, and many of them will wear white clothes or flowing outfits or yoga chic and it might be too groovy for you. Or it might be just the thing. If you are a hip-hop dancer or a rapper, you all should show up and mix up the party. Report back.

Create yourself back into life, for if there is one thing we are all here to do, it's create!

"Art therapy" is redundant. All art is therapy. To create is divine! Get thee doodling!

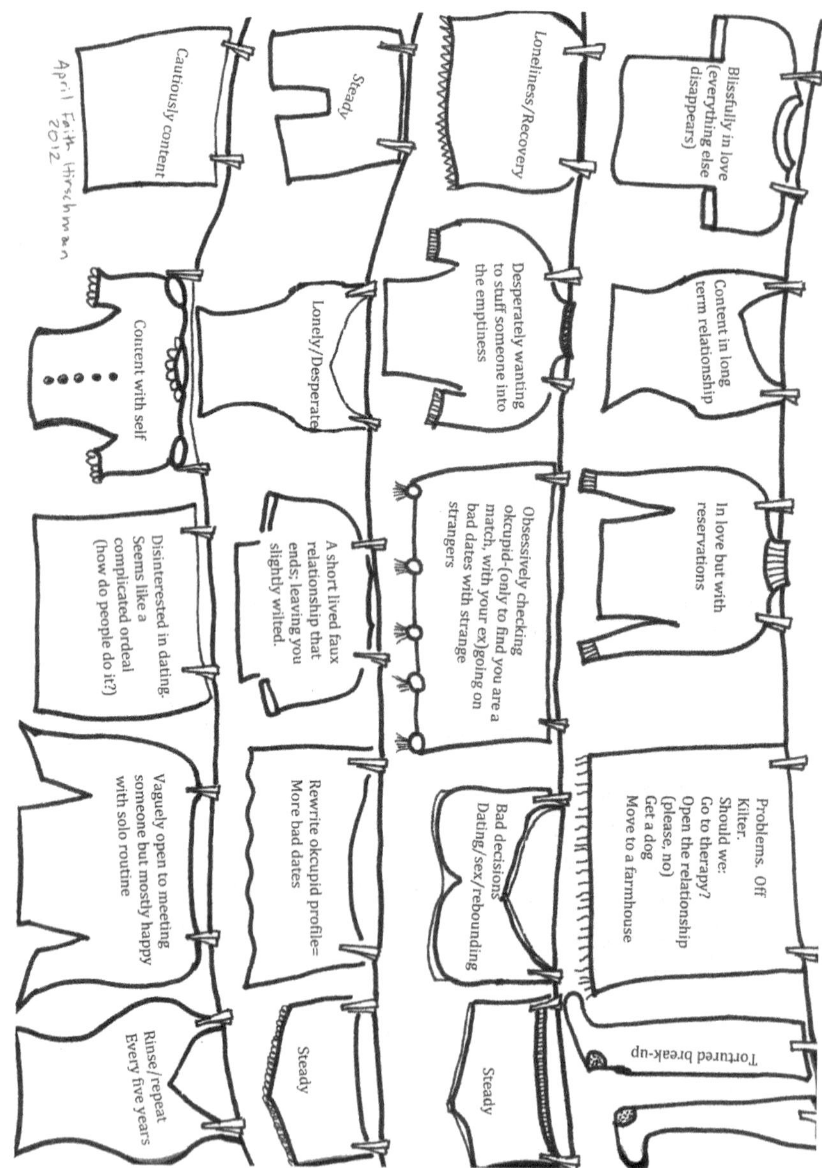

Here is some breakup art I did. Note: this is not my ultimate view on relationships! It was just what I was feeling at the time.

April Hirschman

movie therapy

Well, I'm gonna get out of bed every morning... breathe in and out all day long. Then, after a while I won't have to remind myself to get out of bed every morning and breathe in and out...and, then after a while, I won't have to think about how I had it great and perfect for a while.

Nora Ephron, Jeff Arch, David S. Ward,
Sleepless in Seattle

Sometimes there's nothing to do but escape from it all by watching a movie! You can do this in bed or go to The Picture Show and get the biggest tub of buttery popcorn they got! I recommend getting Reese's Pieces and mixing those into the popcorn so there is a surprise in every bite. If you are weird, like me, you will bring a plastic bag of nutritional yeast (hippie dust) to pour all over your popcorn. Not sprinkle, pour! In San Francisco, many movie houses actually have their own nutritional yeast, that's how weird NorCal is!

But, what to watch? I was going to watch a movie with two friends who recently had breakups. I suggested a Romantic Comedy and they backed away from me and made the sign of the cross. What? I asked. What did I say? Why are you throwing salt over your shoulder? They both said they couldn't watch Rom Coms for months, sometimes years, after a breakup. Oh, of course. How could I have been so naive? I was still watching them after my breakups and wondering why they left me shaking and despondent. I hated those people and the predictable marriage at the end of the film. I would yell at the screen: "I give it three months, tops!"

In Rom Com wedding scenes, even the two "less attractive" friends are matched together in the not-so-subtle hierarchy of

Hollywood-ordained beauty. The only part I like is that many of the side characters are revealed to be GAY in the dance party part of the wedding! But don't get me started about how the queer characters are always the supporting cast! Or that long period of cinematic history where the black friend was promptly killed in the first act or scene. Please let the madness end.

Dear screenwriters: Stop putting weddings at the end of Rom Coms or any movies! For at least like 700 years. Thank you and goodnight.

I find watching Marilyn Monroe movies soothing, as they are so far from real life and her other-worldly dreaminess is just so pleasing. Also her outfits! One time some friends and I watched a Rita Hayworth movie, and we all agreed that it was a surprisingly sexy movie. "But nobody even kissed," I said. "But her dresses," my friend said. "Her dresses."

One winter I watched multiple *Ally McBeal* seasons, night after lonely night. If you missed this cultural phenomenon, you're in for a treat: shoulder pads, third wave feminism, Barry White bathroom musical scenes, Calista Flockhart's pillowy lips and sexy legs, Lucy Liu groping Jane Krakowski.

Still, it was a strange choice, because Ally, the leggy lawyer, ends up sad and alone in every episode. But maybe I felt comforted by that. She was beautiful, smart, talented, self-obsessed, and even she couldn't make love stay. The good thing about a series is you can stay with the characters for a long time. You can tune out your life and tune into theirs for a while. Have you ever watched *Murder, She Wrote*? It's iconic. And many of your favorite actors had cameos back when they were unknown and improperly groomed.

They say when you watch a movie repetitively you are working something out in your life. I watched *Reality Bites* repetitively because it so encapsulated the angst of the time. I learned about working things out through repeat viewings at an Esalen retreat called "Myths, Movies, and Magic." One of the workshop leaders, Jeff Dowd, is the person The Dude from *The Big Leb-*

owski was modeled after! At the end of the workshop, I saw him standing in the doorway, drinking a Caucasian and smoking a joint. He handed me the joint. I don't really smoke, much to my father's disappointment, but The Dude! If The Dude was going to imbibe, so was I. So I smoked Bill Clinton-style. And then I was left with just the roach and I mounted it on a red velvet background inside a gilded frame. Ah, yes, I remember it well.

Where was I? The Talkies! You could watch *The Big Lebowski.* It is certainly no Rom Com and Maude has no intention of marrying The Dude, she's just using him to conceive. She's a rad feminist who makes vaginal art.

I say escapism all the way. I despise most Sci-Fi, but if you love it you should totally watch Sci-Fi.

I find watching *Notting Hill* strangely curative. It's a textbook Rom Com with a damn wedding at the end, though it's just a part of a montage; you aren't forced to watch the nuptials in gory detail. I love that Julia Roberts's character is kind of a jerk. And I love to see super star Hugh Grant pretending to be humble, timid, and all deer-in-the-headlights about being in the spotlight. I find them an unlikely pair, but totally hot together.

"I'm just a girl standing in front of a boy asking him to love her." Rom Com gold! Oh, and all the outfits Julia wears. It's worth it just for that. Oh, and for British accents and the supporting cast. The supporting cast is absolutely brilliant and they all deserve Oscars. Give them Oscars right now! Can you imagine? Send them through Fed Ex! No, UPS. Well, what outfit do you want them to wear when they deliver the belated Oscar? Fed Ex people wear comfy, cozy yet tight-fitting shirts and baggy pants in purple and black; whereas UPS workers wear an old-school brown stiff and starchy uniform. If you were a Girl or Boy Scout and then dropped out of the military and you were just in all those things for the outfits, you would clearly become a UPS driver. If you're a lesbian, you will look good in either outfit so don't fret. In fact when you deliver the next package, you should come up and see me sometime.

I also recommend watching *Girls Just Want To Have Fun, Amelie,* and *Bridesmaids*! I watched *Bridesmaids* in a loop one New Year's Eve, post-breakup, by myself in a ski cabin surrounded by white billowing snow. Only in retrospect do I see why I watched a Rom Com that ended in a wedding. Because it didn't. *Bridesmaids* is not a romance between Maya Rudolph's character and her fiancé. He doesn't actually have any speaking lines. Maybe two, tops. At the big "wedding" scene at the end, Kristin Wiig's character and Maya's character are dancing together to "Hold On," which is not a wedding song at all. It's commemorating the relationship between Maya and Kristen. Check out the movie's poster, do you see how they're sort of leaning towards each other? If I were Kristen Wiig, I too would write a straight romance where Maya Rudolph was pretty much my girlfriend.

Anyhow, this particular New Year's Eve, I ate three different bags of chips in rotation. There were some candies in a jar at the Airbnb and I couldn't decide if they were there for the taking or not, so I was seeing how many I could eat without detection.

Anything with Bill Murray pre-*Broken Flowers* is advisable. You can watch *Meatballs* in its entirety or just the "It Just Doesn't Matter" scene. This could be your new mantra.

A screenwriting teacher turned me on to *An Unmarried Woman.* It was made squarely in the 1970s, but I think it tap dances the timeless. You can tell by the title it's surfing the glorious barrel of second-wave feminism. I find the film refreshing.

I was raised on musicals where if someone needed something, they broke into song about it and everyone around knew the moves and the tune. If you are dancing through a plaza, singing, while a horde of colorfully dressed dancers are behind you doing the same moves, you are winning at life!!! You could sing your way out of any problems even if Nazis were invading your Alpine village. There are too many musicals to even list them here, but of course *Singin' in the Rain* is always a good choice.

I could write a whole other book about movies to watch during breakup recovery. Like *Love, Valor, Compassion, The Intervention,* or any other movie where a group of friends hangs out by the lake and some or most of them are gay. Deep intertwining histories are revealed and played out under the backdrop of a gorgeous mansion, plush green lawns, and a blue infinite lake. Plus, there's tons of sneaking into each other's bedrooms at night! Oh, and Skinny Dipping!

There's nothing like John Cusack as Rob Gordon in *High Fidelity*. This covers so many breakup issues it's as if you're living it with him in real time. He even has rebound sex with a character played by Lisa Bonet (we should all be so lucky). Anyhow, the film is a great dissection of how love can go wrong and how it can be revived. He visits with ghosts of girlfriends past in order to find himself again. To find out what went wrong. He reviews his behaviors and shortcomings, their fights, their compatibilities and incompatibilities. There is a concert at the end instead of a wedding, which I find very democratic. The only thing is, Cusack's character gets back together with his girlfriend, which might infuriate you. But no wedding!

What about watching that darkly absurd British sitcom *Absolutely Fabulous*? What, you haven't heard of it? Watch *Ab Fab!* I Googled it for you (you're welcome) and you can stream it on Hulu! https://www.hulu.com/absolutely-fabulous. In this crazy show, no one is ever in love or in a relationship or breaking up. There are just two zany ladies getting drunk off champagne and vodka, while avoiding work, belittling Buddhism, and saying "Sweetie Darling." Yeah, that's your best bet.

Chant: "It Just Doesn't Matter!" in that sort of exhausted, half-crazed way that Bill's character does in *Meatballs*. Chant it through your hallways, your neighborhood café, greet everyone at work with it, scream it outside that trendy brunch place where people cue up for hours to eat the same Eggs Benedict they could get literally anywhere.

Have your favorite cheer-me-up movie on hand at all times on your TV set, computer, phone, or brain implant. (Is that how people are watching things now?) If you don't have a favorite, refer to the titles above. Yes, there is a list at the back of the book for you. Imagine all the actors are showing up especially to make you smile!

oracle all about it

In the midst of this fast-paced and overwhelming world, it is both comforting and clarifying to have a "wise friend" to consult, in order to understand our role and our gifts, our challenges and our potential. I have found that, every step of the way, the Tarot cards have the uncanny ability to show me exactly what I need to know right now.

Magick Altman, *Magick Tarot*

Are you already an oracle junky with angel cards, Tarot decks, and pendulums strewn about your house? When you walk from one room to another, is it through one of those beaded doorway curtains? That's not really relevant, I was just wondering because I admire when people fully commit to the bohemian lifestyle, even if means beads violently crash into your face when you enter a room. When I visit my friend in Paris at her tiny flat, she has fringe hanging between the only two rooms in her place. It's a lovely sensation as they caress...anyhow, the oracle!

Or perhaps you're not a Spiritual Hunk at all. Maybe when you and your friends have heartaches you suggest going to that new craft beer house, pointing out that the wood on the bar is from reclaimed docks off the pier of Fisherman's Wharf. It would never occur to you to plop on the Ikea carpet and pull out your velvety purple bag of tarot cards. In fact, you don't even know what I'm talking about. At all. "Taro root," you ask, "as in African cooking?" No, not taro root. Though, yum, if it's done right it can really hit the spot.

So let's talk Tarot! Tarot is largely misunderstood at best as fortune telling entertainment, and at worst, as some scary Ouija board séance thing. Yes, you told me about the time you and your friends did the Ouija board and it spelled out the name of a kid at your school and then he almost died. How could I forget?

This brings us to the death card which people are afraid of getting even though it is usually metaphorical and about change rather than a literal prediction of your impending doom. You will die, as scheduled, but the Tarot was not invented to pin-point when. Legit readers like myself are so tired of the played-out scene in the movie where the evil, turban wearing, woman tells you you're going to die. That is as ridiculous as any other ridiculous stereotype.

So, what is the Tarot? It's an artful and delightful way for you to check in with yourself. When you pick a card from a deck, you create a portal from yourself to the infinite universe, where there is so much information to draw from.

I recommend the Motherpeace Deck, The Thoth Deck, or the Voyager Deck. Many curio stores have open decks you can look at. Pick a card and see if you like the imagery. When you choose a deck, get the book that goes along with the deck so you can learn about the symbolism depicted. Some decks have many books about them, so make sure the author's voice and style appeal to you. There's a story that your first deck should be a gift from someone. That's sweet and all but also hogwash. Get yourself a Tarot deck; so much wisdom awaits you.

A good way to start the day is by picking a card in the morning and just responding to the images with your intuition. Then in the evening, read about the card. If the image and sentiment is challenging, you may want to pick another card. The idea being that you got the information from the first card and now you want to know how to move on in a more positive way.

Tarot changes how we think over time, by opening up possibilities and speaking to us directly in the language of art and symbolism. When we are seeing everything through a lens, darkly, it shows us a stunning image of the Universe, and suddenly we are thinking big and bright again. When we feel drained emotionally, we see the pictures depicting cups that have become empty. Our thoughts are mirrored. We have a way to talk and think about the subtle emotional landscapes of our lives. Try picking cards with friends. Maybe you can start to heal from your break-up during a Tarot circle!

Oracle Checklist:

- Tarot Deck
- Pendulum
- Angel Cards (I know many of you are cringing at the word "Angel," afraid your friends will think you've lost your edge. But the cards just contain words like: *Happiness*. I had my baby nephew pick a card with his tiny dimpled hand! He picked *TRUST!* True story, I have witnesses.)
- Inspiration Cards
- Bibliomancy (open a book to any page—there's your oracle).
- Street Oracle (things random strangers say or shout at you during the day). One time after I crossed the street, a stranger said to me: "You made it safely to the other side."
- Though it's not an oracle, I also recommend getting a rose quartz stone and falling asleep with it on your chest, in your hand, or under your pillow. Or put it in your bath! Rose quartz

Tarot changes how we think over time, by opening up possibilities and speaking to us directly in the language of art and symbolism.

is good for heart healing, self-love, and feelings of peace. No, using stones won't turn you into one of them—the New Age airy-fairy Shanti Shanti people. It's a stone from the earth, and it's beautiful, and yes, it does have a vibration (I said it) but just try it, what's the worst that can happen?

breakup **coaching**

Freud: If it's not one thing, it's your mother.

Robin Williams

A great approach to getting support is seeing a life coach or a breakup coach. Coaching differs from therapy in that we don't spend as much time delving into the past. I talk about the past with my clients, of course, because so much of a breakup is about the past, but we also talk about the present and future. I look at the whole person, and see what support they need and then we find ways to get that support. I often give specific suggestions that help bust through old patterns and bring about positive change.

I'm not knocking therapy. I L*O*V*E therapy. And your breakup may have triggered old wounds of abandonment, or not being good enough. If it's time to really delve into your past, then I suggest therapy. I've decided to focus on coaching as it's a different approach and it can be very healing after a breakup. Coaching tends to have a more upbeat and positive tone than therapy. It's not that we cheerlead through the pain or ignore it. We address it, but we usually don't spend the whole time talking about everything that happened to you before the age of seven.

The present and the future have a different vibration than the past. When we do look into the past, we reframe it to help you see how you were doing the best you could, how you were still the heroine or hero of your story even at your lowest point. With the help of coaching, you can come out the other side of the breakup with new perspectives, strength, and empowerment. With a coach, you don't have to just focus on your breakup. You can also talk about making positive steps in other aspects of your life. This helps you see a whole new world of possibilities that this breakup has brought about. It helps you see how this truly was the best breakup ever!

My contact info is at the end of the book. We can do an initial session and see if I am a good fit to be your coach.

bridal dress **therapy**

Rhonda: I've seen your book.
You've tried on every dress in Sydney!
Muriel: That doesn't mean I'm gonna get married.
Rhonda: Then what DOES it mean?
Muriel: It means I WANT to get married.
I've always wanted to get married.

P. J. Hogan, *Muriel's Wedding*

I don't know when I will get married. For most of my life I didn't want to. I wasn't concerned that as a queer/bisexual woman, I couldn't marry another woman for much of my life because I was never interested in the part of marriage where you sign a contract with the state. I always knew I could still have a ceremony and thus be married. That said, I am glad as a taxpayer I get the same damn rights as everyone else.

Before I launch into this chapter I want to acknowledge that it is from a perspective of a femme lady and I know that is only one of many. There are all kinds of brides and grooms and brooms and grides. I hope you will enjoy my bridal therapy journey and write and let me know if you have had one involving suits and ties or loincloths and feather boas…okay, back to the story…

Then, in my mid-thirties, I warmed up to the idea of marriage. I had a wonderful girlfriend at the time. We had been exposed to many of the mistakes of marriage through friends, books, and movies. I wanted us to imbue our own meaning into the ceremony and our commitment to each other. I proposed to her while we were in the bathy waters of Ha Long Bay, Vietnam. We weren't on the boat, we were in the water in the middle of the bay! I struggled to stay on bended knee as I popped the pregunta. She smiled. She talked about a bunch of things. I finally asked her, "So, you haven't really said anything concrete. Is that a yes?" It was not.

Recently, I took matters into my own hands and pulled a "Muriel's Wedding." I went wedding dress shopping to see how it felt even if I was not exactly getting married. I mean, I could get married! I'm just not currently in possession of a fiancé or a girlfriend. I haven't spent a ton of time fantasizing about my wedding. I often think about not wearing a white dress. In *You'll Grow Out of It*, Jessi Klein summed up some of my ambivalence: "It's as if these dresses are designed to erase your individuality, leveling you into a universal symbol of femaleness, like that faceless woman wearing a triangle dress on the door of every ladies' restroom in America."

The hardest part of this was not being honest with the shop owner. I could have admitted that I wasn't getting married. Instead I decided to bend the truth like when Gloria Steinem went undercover as a Playboy Bunny. My reasoning was that I wanted to, for once, really get into the sensation of being a bride planning her wedding. Even as I write this, it sounds so foreign, like

I'm saying I really wanted to know what it felt like to be a soldier preparing for war.

I said I was getting married June 23rd of next summer, giving me over a year to find the right dress (and someone to marry me). My intention was two-fold. One was to see if there is anything inherently therapeutic about shopping for a wedding dress post-breakup. The other was the intention to bring more wedding, proposal, marriage and commitment juju into my life. A solid and logical intention, no?

So just to review, I was born on a hippie commune. Most of the women in my family have had simple weddings at San Francisco City Hall. My parents divorced when I was young. I grew up wanting to be a radical who helped change the world, who didn't want the trappings of marriage, white picket fences, or kids. I still don't want the kids or to be fenced in with them behind anything white. And I don't want some heteronormative marriage with everyone's outdated "roles" adhered to. Marriage for me would be about the pagan ritual and ceremony of unity, about our commitment to holding the chalice of our love sacred, and about having a big old fun party.

Before this particular wedding dress shopping appointment, I had never been to a dress fitting. I mean never. I had never gone to a dress fitting with my best friend or my sisters (though both of them have been married) or an East Coast cousin's. I would be as virginal as the white dresses I would try on. I didn't take anyone with me because it didn't seem right to ask someone to go undercover with me unless we were pretending to be spies! Then I'm sure lots of people would have joined. Spy fantasies aside, I prepared for my (kind of) big day. I only told one friend what I was doing. Because all my references are from movies, I assumed there would be two ladies working at the boutique, one in her early twenties with teenage glowing skin, and an older, elegant lady in her mid-fifties. I imagined they would be very coifed, snooty, and condescending. Mostly I was convinced they would catch me in a lie and humiliate me.

In preparation I had a mani-pedi. I fretted that instead of a fancy lady purse, I was bringing my pineapple-decorated back-pack. I decided my fiancé was named Regis. I practiced saying, "like Regis and Cathy Lee." Then I assumed they would ask about him and I would correct them politely, "her." We were thinking Bali, Hawaii, or Bora Bora for the honeymoon. I have always wanted to stay in one of those huts on stilts in the water. It was a day wedding in Sonoma County. I even put a little "engagement" ring on my ring finger, planning to explain it was from Regis's maternal family's side. I only did a little internet research where-in I discovered that fittings take about an hour, they have shoes you can wear, and you need to start shopping at least six months in advance.

The boutique is located in the Marina District of San Francisco, one flight up from street level. I was entering my princess castle. I have donned Amazon feminist armor against the princess myth my whole life. But I also admire softness, sparkles, gowns, femininity, and pageantry. I am a belly dancer, after all, and we love to get dressed up.

Mary, the owner, greeted me at the front door. She was a lovely lady with a kind face who, I quickly learned, designed all the dresses herself. There were to be no snooty, underpaid salesladies.

We got through the details of the wedding fairly quickly. I treated it like an exam I had just barely studied for. She didn't ask anything about whom I was marrying, the honeymoon, or the ring. Just if it was a day wedding, indoors or out. Outdoor, afternoon and I suddenly found that it would be in a field, but there would be surfaces suitable for heels.

I planned to wear a tight fitting dress above my knee instead of the wide princess gown. But Mary told me that ladies mostly wear those after the ceremony. I guess it's so they can get funky on the dance floor, spill things, and be able to sit down. So I chose the mermaid style with no sleeves. The fitting room was spacious. She closed the curtains behind me and I tried on my first wedding dress. It slumped just a little and Mary came in and did some magic in the back that made it fit perfectly. I slipped on the white silk heels, stood on the round platform, and beheld myself in the large, gilt-framed mirror. I did look elevated beyond a normal human. The dress made me look like I was made for a whole other elegant life. The dress could take me places I had never been with elite people who spoke of elite things!

"That looks great; you have a beautiful body," she said. Even if she says that to all the ladies, it was really nice to hear. It was a strapless white number shimmering with beads over Chantilly lace. The dress had a built-in bodice that was a little restrictive, but not too much. It gave my body a pleasing hourglass shape. I tried to imagine myself on my wedding day. Not knowing what my future fiancé would look like made imagining more difficult. Still, I felt very pleased, content, and excited. I can see why people get caught up in the magic of weddings. It certainly felt like something grand was going to happen, something royal and regal and far removed from everyday life. All these symbols would lead me to crossing over, a rite of passage into a unifying time in my life.

It didn't make me sad or full of longing, as I feared it might. I also didn't feel like I was involved in a farce. I was caught up in the moment.

I learned that brides go commando or wear spanks, that you can sit in the dress if you lift it up in the back first, and you can add a belt on certain styles to give it a new flare for different phases of the wedding events.

The next dress was more flowy and silky and had lace going over flesh-colored fabric so it appeared to reveal more than it did. The belly dancer in me loved how sparkly and glittery it was. Each time I stepped up and down off the pedestal, Mary lent me her arm and I thanked her. We narrowed it down to two dresses. She took pictures of me in the two dresses we both liked the most. She wrote down their prices on her business card. She was curious about my coaching services and asked for my card. I would love to have her as a client, but knew if she called I would have to tell her that I wasn't technically engaged to be married.

I left the boutique feeling happy. It helped that the sun was shining and everyone in the Marina had the glow of wealthy bliss. There were juice shops and healthy bowl cafés. People either wore boutique dresses or lululemon yoga wear. The women had the type of skin my friend Vanessa would say looked so good she wanted to lick it. "I'm not mad about how perfect their skin is, I just want to lick their cheeks." Only time can tell whether the deities of marriage were watching over me and lifting veils and barriers to my love.

I do recommend this practice to anyone who is curious about how it feels to see yourself in a wedding dress. It felt empowering to be a part of this secret club on my own terms, not because someone had asked me to marry them, but because I had chosen to do this act myself. If you try this, you may want to just tell the bridal shop owner that your life coach told you trying on wedding dresses would be therapeutic instead of being an undercover reporter like me. However, the make-believe really enchanted the experience for me.

Your Playlist and Other Musical Things

FIVE EASY PIECES

Once, when I was sad, I said to a kind old priest,
have you learned any secrets to unburden the heart?
and he responded, hum a favorite melody;
wine will always rise to the top of oil.

St. Catherine of Siena

In the classic film *Five Easy Pieces*, starring Karen Black and Jack Nicholson, "five easy pieces" refers to five piano songs played during the movie. I just thought I would clear up that mystery for you.

Songs are written in the language of emotions. Sometimes I can barely listen to any music after a breakup because it can so easily slip me into a somber mood. Music is sentimental by nature. Songs fix themselves in a certain time. The song you heard on the radio as a child brings you right back to that exciting, vulnerable time. Even the song that played repetitively last summer will now always remind you of last summer; it can no longer be just, now. Songs mark first kisses, first dates, first times having sex, even first fights. The worst part about dating a famous musician is their songs will haunt you wherever you go!

My friend and I had both recently split with our girls. We helped each other think of bands that don't talk about love or breakups! They are hard to find. My friend always listened to Talking Heads because they claimed to have songs about buildings and food instead of love and heartbreak. Though they did sneak some love songs in there from time to time.

Under no circumstances should you listen to the first *Bridget Jones's Diary* soundtrack. It's full of mournful songs lik"e "All By Myself."

Certain songs play right on cue when I am in a breakup; usually it's the ditty: "It Must Have Been Love," by Per Gessle of Roxette. Since it came out in the 80s, it's been haunting me for decades now. The lyrics are quite beautiful, though I long ago ceased to actually hear them: "Lay a whisper on my pillow/ Leave the winter on the ground/I wake up lonely, there's an air of silence in the bedroom and all around." This song is always playing on the radio as soon as I enter a car after a breakup.

We have so much control over our music these days that we rarely listen to radio. I, however, still throw myself to the whim of DJs when I drive. For decades, DJ Delilah has been on the air. She is an evangelical Christian with a voice that is smooth and tingly. Salt-of-the-earth listeners call in with their woes, heartbreaks, and wedding announcements, and she puts on just the song they need. Though in my tenure as listener it's usually Peter Cetera's "Glory of Love."

Dear Delilah, my husband and I need a wedding song...
Delilah: Glory of Love.
Dear Delilah, my girlfriend just left me...
Delilah: Glory of Love.
Dear Del-
Delilah: GLORY OF FUCKING LOVE.

Delilah would never swear. Of all my relationships, the one I have with Delilah is the most inexplicable. She is a talking Hallmark card, I hate "Glory of Love," but still, year after year, she keeps me company and makes me feel a little less lonely or sometimes she makes me feel lonelier. It's so confusing!

And why is it that right after you break up, every Adele song follows you wherever you go? She's stalking you! I once went to a wedding right after a breakup, which one should never do. But I did. And I was mostly okay when I wasn't seething with jealousy. Then some of us went to a bar. My mind was jumping from the present to the past with my ex. I was doing my level best to be in the moment. Then Adele came on. I can't remember if she was setting fire to the rain or rolling in the deep, but it was my cue, so I got up and left.

After a breakup, my ex made herself a playlist with songs like "How to Mend a Broken Heart." She said she would share it with me, and I said absolutely not. If that song was any indication of her playlist, it would send me into a tailspin of despair. But others, like you perhaps, may benefit from listening to sad songs for a half hour and then blowing through a tissue box. For some people this is just what you need to feel all the feelings. And as Jonathan Franzen put it: "There is, after all, a kind of happiness in unhappiness, if it's the right kind of unhappiness." Certain songs bring us right into these depths; subtle healing can take place.

I love to listen to Tori Amos' "Cars and Guitars." The brilliance of her music is that you can never figure out exactly what the heck she is talking about. But the emotional resonance is always there, the veiled poetry reveals just enough, she takes you into her "mood indigo" like nobody else. Just as she is singing, "It never was the cars and guitars, that came between us," you are thinking, but maybe it was. And if it wasn't that then it was something else that came between. The option to "keep on drivin" is always there…

We can take charge of our life's playlist, at least at home or with headphones. I have a playlist called the Greatest Love of All. It's helped me through more breakups than I care to admit. My playlist is not breakup compilation but songs of self-love and independence. I like to get up on my bed for the big finish and lip sync with my arms spread wide! For me a breakup is all about re-establishing my relationship with Numero Uno.

Below are my Fifteen+ Easy Pieces:

- "My Way," Frank Sinatra
- "Me Myself I," Joan Armatrading
- "It's My Turn," Diana Ross
- "In or Out," Ani DiFranco
- "I Made it Through the Rain," Barry Manilow*
- "Dancing with Myself," Generation X
- "Man of La Mancha," Linda Eder version
- "Roar," Katy Perry
- "Beautiful," Christina Aguilera
- "Man I Feel Like a Woman," Shania Twain
- "It's My Life," Bon Jovi
- "It's My Life," No Doubt
- "Wide Open Spaces," Dixie Chicks
- "Free Fallin," Tom Petty
- "Greatest Love of All," Whitney Houston
- "Don't Stop Me Now," Queen

*I hear you chuckling that I included a Barry Manilow song here. My sister and I danced in discos to his music, so I've always had a soft spot for this guy. He just came out as gay! Yay, thank you, Barry. We never would have guessed and by that I mean Biggest "No Shit" heard round the world. I am so gay proud of you! Welcome to the club. Once we make it through that rain we can all dry off together in the Temple of Healing. There's a jacuzzi in there! And a disco! If Barry's there, you bet there's a disco and a sequined pants suit. Embrace the syrupy songs of the 1970s. Pour them over your gluten-free pancakes.

- Make your own recovery playlist. Or use mine!

jealousy

The Danish word for jealousy is skinsyg, which literally means "skin-sick." Yikes. Now that we finally found the right combination of horny goat root, rosehips, and egg whites to keep your skin glowing, the last thing we need is for you to break out in an all-over body rash. If you dig deep enough in the confusing etymology of the word jealousy, it includes some vaguely positive terms like "zeal" or "emulation." Hmmm. I know there is something there, I'm just not sure what.

Recently, my friend was swimming in jealousy when his ex-girlfriend shacked up with a hot young guy. She had been cheating on him with said hot guy. Then his ex-girlfriend and the hot young guy got married and pregnant right away! Quelle Bummer! The hardest part was witnessing my friend totally attacking himself and the way he looked. He was caught in the compare/despair paradigm.

There is a long and excruciating musical canon devoted to such feelings. For just flat out badass emoting, Alanis really takes the piñata with lines like "An older version of me/is she perverted like me?/Would she go down on you in a *theater*?" It really paints a visual picture. I think it's the "vivid language" our impassioned 8th grade English teacher was trying to invoke in us. I only just watched the video for the first time. Where is Alanis? Cairo?

"Jealousy," by Natalie Merchant is more of a bedtime lullaby. Lines like: "Is she bright, so well read, are there novels by her bed," spotlight how detailed her thoughts are about her ex's new boo. There's a theme in these two songs by these two artists that I never noticed until I began this investigative reportage. They have imposed themselves into the songs in colorful ways: "Are you thinking of me when you fuck her," and "while she's touching you accidentally do you say my name?"

Ladies, Alanis, Natalie, I applaud you. Of course he was thinking of you when he fucked her and of course he accidentally said Natalie when he screamed out the Big "O."

But you-know-who doesn't really deserve all the attention you are giving them and their new sweet potato. That's time better spent focusing on your amazing self and doing some of the self care things in this very book.

Whoever is with your ex gets the good stuff, but they also inherited all the annoying behaviors and habits that drove you *absolutely mad*. When I was pining over my ex, long after the breakup math said I should be, my friend said: "Yeah, but a lot of the time she was lying on the bed with a pillow over her head and a crushing migraine." It put things in perspective. That was nothing compared to my ex for whom it would be said: "Remember when she didn't pick you up, in your own car, from the airport, twice?" Or "Remember when she was drunk driving in your mom's car, risking totaling it, your lives, and the lives of innocent recently transplanted tech industry hipsters?" With all due respect, whoever is with that ex, well, I pity the fool. Almost as much as I pity the fool I once was.

Jealousy implies there isn't enough to go around. Enough new girlfriends or boyfriends or gender nonconforming dreamboats for everyone. Next time your friend is going to Hawaii, don't say you're jealous—there's enough tropical vacations for everyone. Don't be jealous of the fun of others, there's enough here to go around. As soon as you can, stop thinking about your ex. Look around yourself. Bring yourself back to the moment. No Facebook stalking! The best way to avoid a dark hole is not to go near it.

And as for whoever is with your ex—I PITY THE FOOL.

- If you are obsessing, just wail along with Alanis and get it out of your system.
- If you are feeling the blues, cry it out with Natalie.
- Write a song where you talk about your ex missing you. In dulge yourself. Once you get it out of your system, move back to focusing on Numero Uno.

you can't take that away **from me**

"Hey, you can't take that away from me." That's what my older sister says at a restaurant even if there are only three peas left on the plate. Then she makes a wide sweeping gesture with her hands and says: "We are going to eat everything." At which point the terrified server backs away. Then three bussers try to remove the plates and the whole burlesque starts over again. But the gusto that my family brings to eating out is not what this chapter is about.

You thought this chapter was about dividing stuff up like the sex toys you bought together? But no, it's not. Though my younger sister and I made a movie about that called *Shafted*. It's a sticky topic. *What's that you say?* You're dying to hear more about our lil' movie? Well, the main character seeks legal recourse in retrieving the sex toys she lost in the breakup with her girlfriend. When that fails, she attempts theft that leads her to jail where sexy female inmates make out all around her! It has a happy ending.

I'm talking about the old timey song, "They Can't Take That Away From Me." What a beautiful ballad. Oh, the sweet lingering memories that no one can take away. This song meant a great deal to me after a breakup with a long-term partner. I would hum it to myself in the kitchen. It would float through my thoughts when I walked over the field in Dolores Park where we met.

Your memories are yours. If you let them cloud over with bitterness, then the time of that relationship truly was a waste of time. But if you accept these memories in all their bittersweetness, they become your friends. These chapters of your life are more evidence of who you are.

The song was written by the Gershwin brothers and includes the line "We may never never meet again, on that bumpy road to love/Still I'll always, always keep the memory of..." There's contentment in the tone of the song. A coming to terms that there are really two relationships now: The "bumpy" one that already happened and the one that lives on in memory. The narrator seems content to muse about this relationship, giving it a second life or, as Anaïs Nin would say of writing, "To taste life twice." The refusal to lose those memories is a refusal to lose the essence of love itself.

If you feel ready, journal about some of the good times. If you have a coach or therapist, you can talk about them in your session.

Radical Self-Care

TREAT YO'SELF

The body is a sacred garment. It's your first and last garment: it is what you enter life in and what you depart life with, and it should be treated with honor.

Martha Graham

Self-care can be different for everybody but let's explore some feel-good stuff, shall we?

Here are some rituals of renewal I have adapted from Ayurveda and life.

Olinate

Before you shower, rub your body in sesame oil (in the colder time of year) or coconut oil (in the warmer time of year). Now step in the shower. Be careful you don't slip. Wash your body as usual but focus on pits, face, and privates; don't wash off the oil on your stomach and limbs. After the shower, pat yourself dry instead of rubbing off all those lovely oils. If it's night, I like to take a shower by candle light; it makes the whole thing seem like a mystical ritual instead of just a bright army shower. Just remember to give the tub a scrub down after with some baking soda so no one slips.

Bathing Beauty

The joys of bathing are so numerous that I am sure you know them all. Bathing is good for colds, purification, relaxation, and muscle soreness. Make a little ritual for yourself by lighting candles, listening to music, and lighting incense. Put Epsom salts (about a cup), baking soda (about half a cup), and a few drops of essential oils (such as lavender, ylang ylang, citrus, or whatever you like). You can meditate or just space out. Can you? I'm glad. I usually need to bring a book in there with me. I let my mind follow the story while my body renews itself.

Champi Head Massage

For a brief stint I was giving Indian Champi head massages at my shop on Haight Street. In India, barbers often give men a Champi head massage as part of the service. How nice! So, gentle reader, just put some coconut or jojoba oil on your fingertips and massage around the neck, head, and temples. You can use warm oil and this can double as an oil hair treatment. Just don't put Vaseline in your hair like my friend and I did in seventh grade. It took a week to get that out. Our parents just rolled their drunk and stoned eyes, respectively.

Self-Massage

Massage is a great stress reducer and you don't have to go to a fancy spa to get one. At night, work the meridians that reduce stress: the inner arms, the stomach, the center of the palms, and the center of the feet. There's more about this at the end of the chapter.

Foot Bath Time

In ancient times, when people wore sandals on long dusty journeys, their hosts would greet them with a foot bath! Can you imagine? What a treat. We don't need to think of it as a luxury reserved only for pedicures. It's a simple thing to do. You just need a tub big enough for your footsies, warm water, and perhaps some salts or essential oil. This is great for women who are often taking care of everyone else. Stay seated with your feet in the warm water. You can't jump up and save anyone; you just get to rest. Ahhhh.

Manicure Pedicure

For the growing number of men reading books like this, bless you. Hi, Dad. I know many of you are rolling your metrosexual eyes at me right now, but for the rest of you, mani-pedis are for you, too! From my almost two decades in the massage trenches, I can say that y'all need to get those eagle claws trimmed. That jagged way you are grooming your nails is going to lead to trouble down the road. And as Janeane Garofalo so eloquently put it, "Gentlemen, your heels are so dry!" She suggests just hitting the heel with a dollop of lotion as part of your masturbation session. And if you won't, then let a professional do it. It's cracking like earthquake country down there.

Healing Arts

You could also try a healing modality that is new to you, such as: Craniosacral massage, acupuncture, reiki, a floatation tank (See *Just Float* chapter), or a kirtan chanting group.

Napping

Napping is a part of life in so many countries. The Spanish love their siestas, the Italians take a riposo, and the Chinese nap right on their desks after lunch. A sofa nap is especially luxurious. You can combine acupuncture with napping quite well.

Public napping is popular in our family. Most days after school, my sister collapsed on the sofa with a goofy smile on her face. This sort of drove me mad because I felt like I had to tiptoe around her even though technically I didn't.

She also feels comfortable napping on the couch Thanksgiving Day while everyone makes merry around her. She's an extrovert, so even sleep is something she prefers to do socially. I'm more introverted, and thus a private napper, unless I'm traveling and jetlagged; then I will nap anywhere.

After a nap, I'm spacey and disoriented. Sometimes I call my sister and just say: "Help, bad nap." She says: "Pop in the shower, come over, and I'll feed you." So don't let this spacey period of time turn you off the nap. Putting your head down is a great way to renew yourself in the day. Thankfully, now there is restorative yoga that is really Adult Nap Time! Do I think it's weird that the longest part of this chapter was about napping? No, not at all, why do you ask?

Hot Springs

Hot springs have long been known for their healing, purifying, and detoxifying properties. Don't panic, you don't have to be naked or chant. That's actually a myth about hot springs. Even at clothing-optional resorts you are never required to disrobe down to your bits. Can you imagine enforcing that rule? *Yes, Gertrude, we know you are 88 and grew up in a conservative Christian town, but please strip down to your skivvies like everyone else!* There are plenty that require you to wear a bathing suit. The process of going to hot and then cold water is rejuvenating. You can either talk to people and be social or be in your own space. I like to float on the surface of the water, imagining that the world is supporting me, that for this time I can just let go and be held.

Sauna or Steam Room

Do you have a local spot you can pop into that has a sauna or steam room? When I was a kid, my family and I went to a Long Island beach club where there was a steam room only in the men's locker room. Can you imagine? Because sexism.

If your gym has either of these, why not bring a little basket of spa stuff, and extend your workout time into a pampering session? Or call it the executive workout. I often swim at my gym. Once I'm there and I've showered, I usually am like, *what more do you want from me? Can I hit the sauna?* Bring your coconut oil, favorite face cream, dry brush, you could even do a facial!

acupuncture points for **heart healing**

To talk about acupuncture and heart healing, I have enlisted San Francisco Bay Area acupuncturist Sage Staggs...Take it away, Staggs!

"If you are going through a period of heartbreak or loss, it can be helpful to apply gentle pressure to points on the channels associated with the lung, heart, and pericardium. These channels are located on the inner side of the arms, the soft, fleshy part.

"The lung helps us navigate grief and supports our ability to let go when it is time. A helpful point to massage is Lung 3, Celestial Mansion, located at the midpoint of the upper arm on the outside edge of the bicep.

"The heart is associated with our spirit and infuses our life with inspiration and passion. The point Heart 8, Lesser Mansion, is located on the palm about an inch down, between the ring finger and pinky. Heart 8 balances fire and water, which symbolize joy and fear, respectively. Use this point to move through the difficult emotions associated with estrangement from a partner.

"The pericardium protects the heart, and moderates our intimacy by either allowing us to connect with others, or armoring our heart as a result of painful experiences in relationship. Pericardium 6, Inner Gate, helps to moderate levels of vulnerability so that you have safe boundaries, yet can access deep connection with others. Massage this point by pressing on the inner arm between the tendons, about two inches up from the wrist."

To perform self-massage, locate the above points and press lightly with your thumb and take three slow, deep breaths, then move on to the next point.

your hair **journey**

Some of the worst mistakes in my life were haircuts.

Jim Morrison

It's time to face the real crisis issue: Your hair. Your hair is your crown. It's important and hairdressers are the unsung shamans of the beauty world. Or they can be. I hate getting my hair done. I feel listless, trapped, surrounded by chemicals and alarming hair dryers. But others really see it as a self-care time and I hope you are among them.

I have been interviewing stylists to get a handle on the situation. Most importantly, don't get bangs. Did you hear that? I'm going to turn it up. DON'T GET BANGS! Thank you. There is nothing inherently wrong with bangs. If you already have them then it's fine. Just don't make it part of your breakup hair journey.

One stylist said post-breakup is the worst time to make a major hair change. Though I don't totally agree because there's a long tradition of women getting a killer look-altering hairdo! I wonder whom Meg Ryan had just broken up with when she went for her classic pixie cut. Someone was eating his heart out, I guarantee!

If you can't decide, the best bet is to step back and nurture your hair. Do a simple hot oil treatment. Upkeep the look you already have. Grab a hair mask (a deep conditioning treatment) and use that in lieu of conditioner once a week. Brushing the scalp feels so good. For a good chunk of my childhood I was raised by my dad, so it was fun to make him braid my hair and brush it because he didn't know what the hell he was doing. I know, you grew up in SoHo with two gay dads who totally knew how to do your hair. Stop bragging.

- Draw a picture or print out a picture of your ideal hairdo and show it to some friends before you do anything rash. If you decide to get a look-altering do, bring an advocate along as you would to major invasive surgery.
- Do a hair mask once a week, try a home hot oil treatment, or any other repairing regimens.
- Don't get bangs!
- Try getting a simple trim to spruce things up.

Thoughts! Journals! Mantras!

IT'S ALL IN THE TELLING

Humor is tragedy plus time.

Mark Twain

How are you telling the story of your breakup? And other stories in your life? I'm asking you to tell the story not as victim, but as heroine or hero of your story. Anne-Wilson Schaef said: "You need to claim the events of your life to make yourself yours." It happened. Nothing can change that, so why not tell it in an empowering way? If it comes up in conversation, or just in your own head, language is important and potent.

Let's reframe and reclaim. Cast yourself in the story as the person who truly wanted to love and be loved. You are automatically the star of your story, so why settle for less? Also, pay attention to sentences like: "I always attract losers, committmaphobes, NASCAR drivers, drug addicts." If you keep saying: "I always…" that's sending a message to your brain that never lets you create a new story, pattern, or neural pathway. Your story could begin like this: "I'm a badass. When I am ready to date again, I am going to attract a super-sexy dreamboat who totally gets me."

Write or say a sentence that is a positive summation of where you were with the relationship, and where you're going.

the **diary** of you

Perhaps some day I'll crawl back home, beaten, defeated. But not as long as I can make stories out of my heartbreak, beauty out of sorrow.

Sylvia Plath

If you are someone who, when scaling the Himalayas, sits down under a tree, pulls out your silky fabric-covered journal, unwinds the handspun cording, and writes your heart out on the pages of your memoir-to-go, you may not need to read this chapter. But even if many things in your life never happened unless you feverishly jotted down your FEELINGS about them in a journal, perhaps read on to find your comrades in the Temple of Healing and maybe even some new thoughts on the journal. This is your pillow book. Don't you love the sound of that? A pillow book in Japanese classical literature is a type of private journal or diary. So what to write?

In *The New Diary* by Tristine Rainer, she suggests:

"Everything and anything goes. You cannot do it wrong. There are no mistakes. At any time you can change your point of view, your style, your book, the pen you write with, the direction you write on the pages, the language in which you write, the subjects you include, or the audience you write to."

I keep many journals at once. I'm hard-core into self-reflection. I have a computer journal, a morning pages journal, and a journal that I keep in my purse. So what do my journals contain? Quotes by everyone I meet, things I'm worrying about, things I'm proud of, questions I'm trying to answer, musings, recipes, fortune cookie wisdom, plans of escape. Do you see the theme? Oh, good, please let me know what it is. I've been trying to figure that out all my life.

When I'm trying to find a theme for my various arts, I grasp for this advice from Austin Klean's wonderful little book called *Steal Like an Artist.* He writes, "Don't worry about unity from piece to piece. What unifies all your work is the fact that you made it." So that's what unifies your journal. You wrote it. It's your reflections and the things you chose to cull from your experiences in life. No one ever needs to read it and hopefully you are old enough that your mom is no longer trying to take a peek. If you're like me, you aren't afraid of anyone sneaking a peek as my handwriting is just short of doctor scrawl. They don't teach doctor scrawl in school anymore because everyone types, but in the 1980s it was required. The only "F" I ever got was in handwriting.

I know gratitude and gratitude journals are talked about a lot these days. You would feel grateful if they were never mentioned again. But gratitude is good for your immune system, sleep patterns, and heart! Just ask Science! There's a reason that gratitude is a hot topic dripping with sex. It shifts our focus and our mood even if just for a short while. But if we spend more and more time in gratitude and less obsessing about the past, we are grateful indeed. I suggest grateful lists to my coaching clients and it always produces good results.

Please make friends enough with your handwriting to have a real three-dimensional journal you carry around with you. One of the most famous diarists of all time and my favorite author is Anaïs Nin. She started her diaries as a child and wrote and published them up to her last days on earth. Her insights are profound and often quoted, though she was not writing them for publication. She only chose to do that later. It's full of zingers like this:

Love never dies a natural death. It dies because we don't know how to replenish its source. It dies of blindness and errors and betrayals. It dies of illness and wounds; it dies of weariness, of witherings, of tarnishings.

Now that you're scaling back down the Himalayas, do you see that stunning exotic flower? Why not press it in your journal! Someday in the future during the zombie apocalypse when the internet dies and humans have to talk to each other again, you may really enjoy reading this journal and finding that little memento whose very sight brings you right back to that trek you took a long time ago. I don't actually believe in the apocalypse, I think women of color are going to rise up and take over the world and I honestly can't wait! Oprah will be prominent in this. "Oprah, save us, buy us a car, tell us what to read!"

Write in your journal to rediscover that still, small voice, THE LOVER THAT NEVER LEAVES YOU, the truth that is yours alone. Scribble like nobody's watching. "Surely some revelation is at hand."

If you haven't already… start a journal today or tonight on your computer or pick up one at a paper shop or drugstore.

Put a date at the top of your entry.

1. Free write to your heart's content.

2. If option # 1 feels overwhelming, then list:
   - 3 things you are grateful for
   - 3 things you are proud of about yourself
   - 3 self-care things you are going to do this week

   I promise if you just let your "voice" come out through the pages of the journal you will cultivate a deeper relationship with yourself.

3. If you still feel stuck, get the book, *The New Diary*, by Tristine Rainer. There is plenty to inspire you in those pages.

let's **mantra** again like we did last summer

Mantras don't work, you say? Mantras are phrases people in India and Northern California chant while they align their chakras? Well, maybe so. But here's the thing. There are negative mantras in your head speaking to you all day. Sometimes they say: *Get out of bed, you're so lazy!* Or: *You always say the wrong things.* Or: *You're not good enough.* Or: *You don't fit in.* This is the voice of your inner critic or gremlin. He or she is a real killjoy, wet blanket, and general bummer. One way to not let the internal turkeys get you down is to have a different statement in there to even out the score.

You can call it a mantra or an affirmation. So much of what we deal with after a breakup is ourselves. In partnership we had many things to distract us. So I think now is as good a time as any to say really nice things to yourself. A mantra can be as simple as that. Louise Hay says, "Plant healing thoughts and ideas that support you in developing self-confidence and self-esteem, and creating peace of mind and inner joy."

You can repeat the opposite of what your gremlin says. If he says you are fat and lazy, you can say, *"Actually I'm gorgeous and I just worked eight hours."* But let's go a little deeper, shall we? All the way down to the root of it all, self-love. Remember when I asked you to say an affirmation every night? No? That's okay, now is the time to start. Lie down in bed and put one hand on your heart and one on your belly and say inside your head,

"I love myself unconditionally. I accept myself completely. I am whole, I am perfect, I am complete."

It took a while for the vibration of these new thoughts to really take root in my consciousness. *It took saying it every night for months.* Just like strengthening your immune system, strengthening your emotional pathways takes time. Slowly I found a calm, grounded, self-loving place in myself. That is where I always land. Remember when Whitney told us to "find your faith in love?" This is a way to halt the free fall into self-doubt and self-criticism. You can also do what Hay and many others call Mirror Work. You can say your self-loving affirmations while looking in the mirror. Practice again, and again, and you can actually rewire your neural pathways.

Still not buying it? You think it's a waste of time? Just trust me on this one. Fake it until you make it.

Text or email eight friends and family members. Have them send you three words that describe you. Tell them your life coach told you to; or that it's part of the healing work you are doing in your self-help book. Then sit back and watch as the beautiful healing words pour in. Put them on one page, print them out, and put them on your wall or journal. Or write them out by hand in colored pens. Just look at you!

No, I'm not sure why your uncle wrote: gloomy, depressed, anxious. Don't invite him to Thanksgiving! He's one to talk, being a professional hacky sacker and full-time stoner. But your aunt and best friend said really nice things. Or they will. Text 'em right now! Now turn these words into affirmations about yourself.

- Say the self-love affirmation every night.

eternal sunshine of the spotless mind

How happy is the blameless vestal's lot!
The world forgetting, by the world forgot.
Eternal sunshine of the spotless mind!

Alexander Pope

Don't we all wish we could erase certain painful memories or whole relationships as in the movie *Eternal Sunshine of the Spotless Mind*? That we could interrupt the voice that pleads: "If I wouldn't have started that last argument. If I wouldn't have asked him or her to clean up that mess. If I wouldn't have had needs and wants."

Don't watch *Eternal Sunshine of The Spotless Mind* right after your breakup. Now is not the time. Okay, you can watch it if you really need to cry it out, face the heart of darkness, and come out the other side. But at least watch it with a friend. Personally, I think it's too soon.

Don't die your hair blue like Kate Winslet's in the movie. Just because blue looks good on Kate Winslet doesn't mean it's the right look for everyone. She has enormous eyes, usually only found in cartoons, so of course her hair would look good blue or literally any other color. Those cheekbones!

I am sentimental, and I tend to replay scenes in my head from past lovers, so this movie really got me. It would be swell if we could erase some of the heartache. If only we could get our hands on the nepenthes drug of Homer's *Odyssey*. It was said to banish grief and trouble from a person's mind.

So what do we do with all these memories that so quickly can turn to distracting intrusive thoughts that zap us out of the moment?

When these intrusive thoughts attack, here is your prescription:

- Pause
- Breathe
- Tell yourself: *That was the past and I am letting it go with love.*
- Come back to the present of wherever you are.

When in doubt, do a journal entry and bleed your feelings onto the page. Maybe if you write out some of these stories, you can finally put them to rest.

the best letter you **never sent**

I know, I know, you savvy, new-age Goddess/Hunk/Gender nonconforming Dreamboat. You've heard it all before. You write a letter which you don't send, wherein you air all your grievances, heal, and move on. But have you actually done it? I didn't think so.

Open up your computer or your locked diary and start composing the best letter you never sent. I am not just preaching here. I have done it. There is nothing to censor here. You can let it rip. You can even name and blame. Or you can show all the tenderness that it just isn't safe right now to show to you-know-who. Ramble on and on. There is no limit. Feel ALL the feelings. FEEL everything. I have even written a letter from my ex addressed to me where they said all the things I wish they would still say to me about how sorry they are about ruining us. I sent this letter to myself and it took over a week for the mail carrier to deliver it. I wondered if it had been lifted off to some magical epistolary limbo. I liked that it took a while to come back to me. I wondered if it would ever return. When it arrived, I read it as if for the first time, and felt soothed by the words that were and were not my own.

Maybe somewhere in never-neverland there is a postal worker who delivers, energetically, all the unsent letters of the world. On some level these letters are delivered and you will feel subtle shifts in yourself. In some way she, he, they may feel them as well. Separation is the greatest illusion of all. All things are felt by the collective unconscious.

Write a letter you will not send to your ex. And/or write a letter from your ex to you.

can you **picture this?**

The power of visualization cannot be overstated! Even when I go to the gym and shoot hoops all by myself, the ball never goes in the hoop unless I picture it in my mind. *Did you just flip to my author photo? Why so shocked that I shoot hoops?*

In *Simple Abundance,* Sarah Ban Breathnach (also a great quote hunter) reminds us, "Our subconscious mind cannot distinguish between what's real and what's imaginary (which is why creative visualization works)."

Take some breaths and imagine yourself in one year being happy again with the simple pleasure of life. Visualize the life you want to create. How does it smell, taste, touch, and feel? What are you wearing? Where are you living? Who is in bed next to you? Paint a vivid picture of your life in one year.

Put the book down. Do it now.

For those of you who dislike visualizations, there are plenty of other tools here for you to try.

III

In The End

WHAT TO EXPECT WHEN YOU'RE BOUNCING BACK

Okay, sailors and rebels. We have some more time to spend together. If you skipped right to this page for some reason then, well, HELLO THERE! If you have been bouncing along chronologically, then things are winding down, but there is still more to do together. And I know that just because we are getting to the end of this book it doesn't mean that you don't still want to strangle happy couples or kick cats. It's an up and down road. Okay. Let's keep going! But first…Letting Go.

Here are some tips from author Susan Sontag's journal to help you on the healing journey:

> "Regenerative experiences:
> Plunge into the sea
> The sun
> An old city
> Silence
> Snow-fall
> Animals"

Love The One You're With

THE LOVER WHO NEVER LEAVES YOU

The only childhood truly deserving of the title "privileged" is one which imbues someone with a capacity to be a friend to themselves.

Alain de Botton

Sometimes my family and I get together and create a circle. We sit on a blanket in Golden Gate Park. If it's 420 Day, and we are in a silly mood, we attempt to recite Indian chanting from our commune days while smoking an imaginary joint. The fun is in the gesture of holding it and passing it around and cough-talking. Sometimes it's with my whole nuclear family and sometimes it's with just my mom and two sisters.

In my late teens, we gathered with all the women in my family at our little house near Occidental. We sat in our circle and everyone said what was coming through them at the time. My older sister talked about the lover who never leaves you. (Are you noticing a theme? My sisters are amaze-ovaries). That lover is with you throughout your days. They show up in the mirror every time you look, even if you don't say the kindest things when your eyes meet. That lover can be so easily taken for granted, discarded, and abandoned. We are taught to find love and fulfillment through partners, food, drugs, entertainment, and porn. Just about anywhere but here, in our very center.

If you are truly at home in your thoughts, in your own body, you can see that you are already perfect and your perspective on life will change. You are not that project you keep abandoning and feeling compelled to improve. In *Awakening Loving-Kindness,* Pema Chödrön writes: "When people start to meditate or to work with any kind of spiritual discipline, they often think that somehow they are going to improve, which is a sort of subtle aggression against who they really are."

You are not that project you keep abandoning and feeling compelled to improve.

I work with my life coaching clients on their inner critic, that nagging voice that is always telling us we aren't good enough. And then I work with them on cultivating a kind, loving voice that says things like: "It sounds like you are upset, sweetheart; what do you need right now? Don't worry, I'll take care of you." Can you imagine if a sweet, nurturing voice was there to greet you instead of that killjoy who is often belittling your best efforts?

When I took a Geographic Cure to Spain post 9/11, I was at the lowest point I had ever been in my life. I lost my first girlfriend, my dance troupe, my home, and all that was familiar to me. I went to Madrid in the winter to start a new life. One should never start a new life in Europe in the winter! But I was too young to know that. I was walking alone in the metro. Most of my time there was walking alone as everyone else was bustling by with their friends and family. The metros are stark and cold and smell of stale cigarettes and loneliness. I felt loneliness deep into my very being. I looked down to notice that I had begun holding hands with myself. I walked a long way with that unfamiliar and uncustomary gesture. Somewhere deep inside me was the lover who would never leave me, and in my darkest hour she had reached out and grasped my hand.

Try today, this week, and all your days on this earth to replace the nag with a curious loving voice. This loving self is you, and will always be with you. You can give it your own name or a name that you love. The more you organize your life around this center, this self-love, the less life will drag you down.

like the sky **holds** the earth

See if you can soften around it, holding the soreness very softly and spaciously, like the sky holds the earth.

John Welwood

If you are ready for a very tender, slow-paced self-help book, I recommend *Perfect Love, Imperfect Relationships* by John Welwood. All self-help books are companions while you grieve, or grow, or recover.

"There is nothing like relationship to show us where we are frozen and shut down, where we have trouble making contact, where we are most afraid, and where we refuse to accept what is." A breakup is one big acceptance speech for what is. Denial is usually acknowledged as the first stage of grief. So where are you right now? If it's denial, then it's in the raw beginning stages of shock and disbelief. At every stage, the best we can do is soften around our hurt and just hold space for our grief like the sky holds the earth.

the you in you

I was introduced to the concept of the you in you in the book *The Hotel New Hampshire*, by John Irving. What a unique read! Franny Berry is one of the main characters, played by Jodie Foster in the film adaptation. After she is raped, her friend Junior Jones tells her that that person didn't get "the you in you." And nothing can. We always have something uniquely ourselves that no one can ever steal from us. After a breakup we tend to lose sight of this. We feel rejected and unlovable and can't remember why anyone was ever in love with us in the first place. Our doubtful self says: "Maybe they never were."

Finding out who we truly are is like a slow unfolding spiral; like the spiral that whittles off an apple's skin, revealing the sweet white fruit below. It's so easy to want to be someone else. Cary Grant said: "Everyone wants to be Cary Grant. Even I want to be Cary Grant." He was born Archibald Leach and perhaps he remained Archibald Leach all the days of his life. He walked a complex tightrope between these shifting personas. Perhaps you aren't one of the most famous actors of all time and you don't have to deal with that. Nevertheless, you should watch *Holiday* with Cary Grant and Katherine Hepburn. Young Archie was in the circus and those two doing somersaults brings me inexplicable joy! I've added it to your movie list. Katherine seems like a dame who was stubbornly herself to her last breath. We can all take a page from her script.

Finding out who we truly are is like a slow unfolding spiral; like the spiral that whittles off an apple's skin, revealing the sweet white fruit below.

Sometimes reconnecting to your authentic self is as simple as asking: *What would I do in this situation?* That's right, you! I trust you. The world trusts you. Tell 'em your life coach friend said it was okay to just be you and trust yourself.

I've read several of Carrie Fisher's books and watched her *Magical Drinking* show. It sounds like being Princess Leia was the best worst thing that ever happened to her. Or maybe it was the best thing at the time, followed by the worst repercussions. Although according to her diary, at the time, it didn't sound that great either. Harrison Ford, you old so and so! In all the excitement and drama, when the smoke cleared it was hard for anyone to see *her*. They saw a space princess. Countless men told her, to her face, that they masturbated to her in their adolescence. As glamorous as that sounds, she wasn't thrilled with it. At the end of *The Princess Diarist* she addresses the question: "Whom do you think you would've turned out to be if you weren't an intergalactic princess?"

"I'd be me.
You know, Carrie.
Just me."

It's nice work if you can get it. To be just you. And you can. May the force be with you. Speaking of the force, did I ever tell you about the time I got to tour Skywalker Ranch? It's top secret there, and when they talk about the movies they're editing, it's all in code. The lands are gorgeous and palatial and there's a farm and a vineyard. All the people who work there seem like happy workers right out of *Toy Story*. Maybe it's better to be a nerdy editor inside a soundproof room all day than a superstar. Hard to say, as I can't imagine living in a cave or like a princess. I'll just stick to being myself. *Just me.* It's all I can do not to tell you: "Be yourself, everyone else is taken." Shoot, it just came out, like a tic. I'm sorry, that one's really played out. Think of a new one, write it in your journal, and report back.

the power of one

There is a road, no simple highway between the dawn and the dark of night and if you go no one may follow that path is for your steps alone.

The Grateful Dead

Whether you are healing from a breakup as a single person, or someone who is already in a new relationship, now is as good a time as any to look at the ridiculous obsession with coupledom. For all America's mantras about "rugged individualism," we still elevate couples above all other forms of being. Popular music is often variations on the theme of "I can't live if living is without you." All these songs locate love outside yourself and project it on the other, often an other who is just out of reach. Obsessive love is ritually normalized in the lines of songs and the plots of movies. In the way conversation amongst the spunky ladies of *Sex and the City* came to an abrupt halt at the suggestion that they talk about something besides relationships with men.

Everyone is experiencing triumphs and hardships in their lives, whether single or coupled. When we are single, we have the freedom to do what we want when we want. We aren't aligning ourselves with our partner's wildly different desires or arguing about the intimate details of something. Sometimes, we really get our shit together at these times and sometimes we really fall apart.

I was in my early twenties when I first noticed how socially unacceptable it was to be the odd woman out. Though I am not supposed to comment on it, some have considered me fairly easy on the eyes. At this time, despite this and my other charms, I was single for the stretch of time known as the college years where everyone's copulating like rabbits and discovering their bisexuality. When I hung out with my straight couple friends, my presence sparked a subtle discomfort. The men wanted to know why I was spending so much time with their ladies, was I hitting on them? The women wanted to know why their men were giving me attention, was it just talking, or flirting? My place was not clear in the social stratification of couples, and I was cast as a scarlet woman bound to wreak havoc on the constellations of my "normal" friends.

Later, when I was in my thirties, single and at a queer event, many well-meaning friends would whisper, "So is there anyone here catching your eye? I can wingman for you." The worst part is that I have done this to my friends, too. It tends to single out the single person instead of helping them socialize. When my friend said it to me recently, I wasn't in a flirty mood. I was just enjoying a time in my life of not looking.

The self-inquiry I have been able to do as an unattached person has been priceless. I am proud of solo endeavors I have undertaken that represent brave independence. I have traveled many countries of the world by myself, and often without the built-in social comfort of a school or group tour. You really locate yourself when you travel alone in the world. You find out what you are made of. I have walked through canopied Turkish streets flanked by huge jars of olives and coin scarves catching the light in their tiny mirrors. I belly-danced spontaneously at a Balinese festival. I walked alone in Madrid and Kathmandu when everything was dark and quiet. I have gone places alone and ended up having a banquet with people I only met a few hours prior. In our different languages and backgrounds, I was able to find commonality and connections with strangers.

The loneliest times have been the deepest ferments of my character. Because I would ask myself, "Okay, you are lonely in the south of France, looking out at the bluest blue water of La Calanque de Figuerolles, eating a chilled shrimp salad with seventeen ingredients; do you want to go home?" The answer was always "no." I knew that this sadness would eventually melt back into joy, as is the ongoing experience of life.

I wanted to know myself without the familiarity of my city block, my social scene, my country, my language. I've had the deepest insights from these places of standing strong on my own. I have found strength in my ability to take care of myself, to make all the decisions of life on my own, and to know myself as you only can without someone constantly there to comment on it.

When I am not in a relationship, I take more classes, expand my social circle, go more places alone, and attend more art openings, poetry readings, and dance shows.

Though at times, I want to stubbornly defy this, I know that for me, my life has purposely been bestowed with times of great love and togetherness and times of the solo sojourn. There is a pattern of crashing and releasing, of opening and closing, that follows the rhythms of the natural world. I am a lover at heart and always want to be in love. But I needed those times of being single to find the path that's for "my steps alone."

You don't have to call yourself "single," by the way. It's not always the most empowering title. You can say: "I'm keeping my options open", or "I'm enjoying alone time right now."

There are other times, especially as the years pass, when I get unexpectedly sad about my "single" status. A guy friend accompanied me on a shopping trip to Bed Bath & Beyond not too long ago. I was looking for curtains and a new bedspread, a whole new color scheme for my room and therefore my life. As I touched the colored and patterned fabrics, something was missing. My partner was missing. Where was she? Why weren't we making these decisions together? I became sad and despondent. I finally understood what the "beyond" in Bed Bath & Beyond meant. I was beyond and my friend slowly escorted me out of the store. I was holding a sad little pan in my hand instead of a whole bedroom concept that would magically turn me into a whole new woman.

If you look around, you will see that the unattached people in your life are living amazing lives, as are the coupled. And yes, some single people are very lonely. And some of the coupled folks are compromising too much and miserable and lonely. It's funny how, even when someone is in a dysfunctional marriage, they read as at least being lovable. At least someone wanted to marry them; whereas curiosity grows around a single person. Why are they single? Avoiding the deeper question of why is that person willing to be in a dysfunctional marriage to avoid being single?

Despite the fantasies of marriage, despite how it's chanted into the hearts of little girls as their ultimate purpose, our ultimate purpose is much more complex than that. So where are your steps alone taking you?

We all have to face this same question, and since nobody said it better I'll just go ahead and cue *The Invitation:* "I want to know if you can be alone with yourself and if you truly like the company you keep in the empty moments."

Close Encounters of the Ex Kind

WANTING CONTACT (WITH YOU)

There you stand before me, all that fur and all that hair Oh, do I dare, I have the touch wanting contact, I'm wanting contact I'm wanting contact with you.

Peter Gabriel

I really wanted to call this chapter: *All That Fur and All That Hair,* but I'll save that for another book. I need some time away from my ex after the breakup. I've mostly taken it. But not always. In a recent breakup, I indulged in some post-breakup sex. It all started when I was leading a lesbian matchmaking event. The event wasn't going so well. It was right after the Trump election and everyone's nerves were rattled. No one was particularly in the mood for flirting. So I started drinking wine and Champagne to take the edge off. I asked the French proprietor which to drink first. He said first the Champagne, then the wine. I followed his advice. But as I don't really drink, I'm the lightest of the lightweights. Soon I was drunk texting my ex: "So breakup sex is out of the question right?"

"No, it's not out of the question," was her rather quick reply. So we hooked up a few times, each time a little worse than the one before. The sex itself was good, it was always good with us, but all the emotions and interactions surrounding the sex were heart-wrenching. We just went back and forth between blaming each other and feeling sad and feeling bad.

Calling and talking to her would always make me cry because she was finally doing things in her life that I wanted to be a part of. It's like I was watching a movie I had always loved, but now something was missing, and it made me feel lonely to the core. Finally, after this period ended, my healing could properly begin. Every couple is different. I can't really prescribe here. At times, many times I'm sure, you want contact. You want to see what condition your condition is in. But you often need space for your one to become two again. You each need to go into your own hermit's cave to heal. Whether you will reunite as friends is anyone's guess. It helps if you were ever friends to begin with. See if you can give yourself about three months without making contact with your ex. Maybe when you meet up again, you can have a breaking-up ceremony together to bring closure to the experience.

In *I Know What I'm Doing and Other Lies I Tell Myself*, Jen Kirkman has some strong opinions about contacting your ex. If a friend says:

> "Should I call her?"
>
> "No! The answer is always no to the question 'Should I call him/her?' Nobody should call anybody."

When you were in a healthy relationship, your lover was there to comfort you when a colleague, family member, or friend hurt you. Now you and your ex are both in pain at the same time. There is a feeling that you should be able to hold each other, commiserate, cry together, have letting-go sex. We want to be comforted by our ex, the one person who can't offer us any comfort. A road has forked. Paths have diverged. It's time to make peace with what singer Katell Keineg calls: *What is and what can never be.*

We often need comfort from our friends and family instead of our ex. On some level our ex has triggered the immense pain we are feeling. Therefore, just as we are trying to be soothed by them we may feel angry toward them. It also may make us impossibly sad to see a person who, in all ways, looks like our love but is not, somehow. Being in their presence can be a stab to our hearts, and a reminder of the finality of the end of the relationship. The breakup that never quite happens and tries to shift right into friendship usually just prolongs the inevitable sadness of loss.

My screenwriting teacher used to say that when you watch a dinner scene in a movie, it's the silent character, the one who is observing it all, who actually has the power in the room. Whether it's the stoic father or the petulant teen, this rings true. Your silence stops the dialogue between what was and what is. It lets your ex guess about you and then eventually stop guessing and start moving on. They see your conviction by all you don't say. That deafening silence that is unheard is the sound of your freedom, your new beginning.

Still not sure how to proceed? If that person still makes you feel sad and hurt it could be a sign that you need more time and space before seeing them.

Perhaps in the future you will indeed be friends. It's a cliché in the lesbian community that all one's friends were once one's girlfriends. There's a bit of this in every community perhaps. But initially, going from partners to friends is a demotion. Only time can allow you to transform into what you will be to each other.

is social media **stalking** for you?

People may use Facebook to keep tabs on an ex-partner's current activities by checking on his or her status updates, wall posts, comments, and photos; even if one is no longer Facebook friends with an ex-partner, publicly available information—such as a profile photo and list of friends—can still provide a rough approximation of the ex-partner's ongoing activities.

From a report published in the journal *Cyberpsychology, Behavior, and Social Networking*

Well, the short answer is no, online stalking isn't for you. But boy, is it hard to resist. I had a very sweet young man as my coaching client who married a woman he truly loved. But he was also having trouble letting go of his ex, a woman whom he had had a very passionate relationship with. He was doing fine until a mutual friend let him look at her Facebook page. He saw that she was getting married, and all those images put him into a full tailspin. He came to me so we could work on finally letting go of her so he could move on and be more present with his wonderful wife. He needed to stop looking at their old pictures. This could be a good time to unfollow or unfriend their Instagram, Facebook, and whatever social media is popping up this moment. If you are checking your ex's Facebook page too much, I recommend blocking it.

Once this kind of passive stalking wasn't even possible. You had to really make an effort to stalk an ex. You had to drive to their house or place of work. Let's try to keep it as dignified as possible. If you must visit their pages from time to time, I totally get it. With any luck you could discover what author Francesca Serritella talks about in regards to her ex: "I want them to move on (slowly), date other people (after I start seeing someone first), and be (almost as) happy (as I am)."

Partially, the search is just to remind yourself that they were once yours, that they didn't vaporize, that they still exist, and that they have 10,000 new posts and photos to prove it. But what if that stalking time, where you feel kind of terrible about yourself, was spent just spending time with yourself or friends, doing something you enjoy like making sauerkraut, feeding snakes, or taking your niece or nephew to see the new cartoon everybody's talking about? Let's direct that beam of love right back onto number one.

- Social Media—check in with yourself before you look at your ex's page. What do you want to feel?
- What are you hoping to get out of seeing their latest pic—check in with your body after you look at their media. How do you feel now? Do you want to feel this way again?
- Block them.

hug and **release**

What if on some moonless unenchanted evening you should run into your ex? Not five years from now, but three weeks from now? What if, like Harry in *When Harry Met Sally,* you are singing "The Surrey with the Fringe on Top" in front of Ira?! I apologize to all young'uns who haven't seen the movie, but you should, it's timeless. Bless you, Nora Ephron. Running into our ex puts the fear of fear into our bedraggled hearts. Sometimes whole social structures have a big, long crack in them, like an earthquake has severed the shared friendships into yours, mine, and ours. Sigh. Super Bummer.

It's really sad when you haven't seen your ex in months, and you wonder if you should text them to see if they are going to a particular social event you used to share. There's no easy answer here. This came up recently. I decided not to text, keeping my vow of silence. She didn't show, so all was well. It reminded me that what we worry about is not what we need to worry about. It's the unpredictable crap that really gets us.

That said, what about when you are in that terrible gray area where you think they might be there and you kind of want them to be there and see what happens. No, no, no. As they say in AA, "If you don't want to slip, don't go where it's slippery." The worst is to just fling yourself into their path with no plan. If you think you might run into them, reconsider going. If you must go, think about what you will really gain from this interaction.

Chances are you're not going to run into your ex when your hair is coifed, your clothes are new and shiny, and your socks match. You will probably be shuffling along in the No-One-is-Supposed-To-See-Me-I-Am-Just-Moving-My-Car outfit. Your pajamas, in other words. But there they are, hopefully not with a younger, cuter version of you on their arm.

But should you run into your ex, and you are on somewhat decent terms, like the kind where you actually say hello and even hug as a greeting, make sure you hug and release. That's right. No long, drawn-out hugs. No eye gazing and getting all misty about what might have been. Never let them see you sweat! You broke up, remember? Hug, release, and walk away, on to your new, amazing ex-free life!

Here's the thing. If you do run into an ex, I hope it's in a field. Not the kind we had keggers in as teenagers where you woke up with straw in your thong or boxers. The kind Rumi alludes to:

"Out beyond ideas of wrongdoing and rightdoing,
there is a field. I'll meet you there."

Better Luck Next Time

Yes, this section only has one chapter in it. So? Who made up these rules? Don't boss me, literary convention.

the thesis statement is **true**

When someone shows you who they are, believe them the first time.

Maya Angelou

Everyone tells you their Thesis Statement at the beginning of a relationship. It is often quite clear and direct: "When I have a good thing, I always sabotage it." This is what an ex said, and this is exactly what she did. She did it thoroughly and it began immediately. Another one could be: "I'm afraid of commitment" or "I'm not looking for anything serious" or "I don't want kids, ever." "I have been hurt badly in the past and can never love again." It's true. The thesis statement is always true. ALWAYS BELIEVE THE THESIS STATEMENT AND ACT ACCORDINGLY. I would apologize for capital letter yelling at you, but women apologize too much.

A thesis statement is defined as: *A short statement, usually one sentence, that summarizes the main point or claim of an essay, research paper, [or person's relationship desire], and is developed, supported, and explained by the text by means of examples and evidence.* Did your ex give you their relationship thesis statement? Were there examples and evidence of it in their behavior? The purpose of a thesis statement is to prove that it's true. You don't have to be particularly scholarly to do this.

At a younger stage of your life, if, for example, your boo wants kids and you don't, maybe it's not such a big deal to ignore the thesis statement, because this is an experimental time in life and sometimes people's ideas about having kids change. And then again, sometimes they don't. If you get only one takeaway from this book, then I've failed completely. Just kidding. I hope you retain more than one, but if it's one, then: please believe the thesis statement. Don't bargain, ignore, regress, plead, hope, or manipulate. It won't go away. It's who they are and what they want. It's crazy to think you will be the exception to the rule. I know because I have practiced this brand of crazy myself. Ignoring the thesis statement can be intimately connected to abandoning yourself in order to be loved. Are you going to ignore this fire-truck-sized red flag, and go on building your life with someone who obviously can't sustain love? No! You are not the exception. You are the rule.

Here's a tricky loophole in the Thesis Statement. Sometimes people's Thesis Statement contradicts their present circumstances or past track record. For example, someone says they want to get married and have a family but they live in a one-bedroom trashed apartment, don't own a pet, and have plants dying on the kitchen windowsill. Perhaps they are also in punishing credit card debt. None of these are signs of family stability. Another case in point is someone who has never had a good relationship. Hey, this can be true and you can be their first, but you probably won't be. They will need to have gone to therapy, seen a relationship coach, or done some other active intervention. These folks may not have a place in their heart for your love to land. They can keep up with the good vibes for a while, but eventually they may cut you loose and continue their pattern of dating people on their messed-up wavelength. Most people can keep crazy in their pocket for a couple of months.

And yes, there can be positive thesis statements like "I have so much love to give and I can't wait to find the right person," "I am excited to share my life with someone." If you both share these positive thesis statements (and there isn't glaring contradictory behavior) then Mazel Tov! That's great. Just don't sweep the destructive ones under the rug because, at some point, you will trip over all the crap that has accumulated there. You have much greater adventures in store than tripping over some crap under your damn rug, no?

And Now Back to Me

NEW RULES

Anaïs Nin said: "Had I not created my whole world, I would certainly have died in other people's." Ani Difranco sang: "Who said I like right angles/these are not my laws/ these are not my rules." So make your own rules. Make your own world! Imagine it, Yoko Ono and John Lennon style. If you are keeping a journal, write it in there. Otherwise simply write it on a piece of paper. Keep it on your altar, under your pillow, by your bed, or in your bag.

My rules are as follows:

Rule #1
I will feel good moving my body every day*

Rule #2
I won't date alcoholics

Rule # 3
I will live part-time in a warm climate.

- Make a list of your Three New Rules
- If it's not too soon, also make a list of rules about whom you will date in the future. And whom you won't date.

* Doesn't "Feel good moving my body every day" sound better than "I will exercise every day?"

everybody, lives back!

Wasted love! God, I wish I could get it back!

Joel Schumacher, Carl Kurlander, *St. Elmo's Fire*

One New Year's Eve my friends, sisters, and I declared it: Everybody, Lives Back in the New Year! It was a collective friend group sentiment after a wave of breakups. My younger sister had just broken up with a real energy sucker. When the smoke cleared, she was glad he was gone. She encouraged us all to review the year and ask ourselves if we had given away our power, our voice, or our lives. Well, this was the year we were going to get our lives back. So we got into a pie fight in her kitchen. We sprayed each other with whipped cream. When we ran out of whipped cream, we sprayed each other with olive oil cooking spray which IS NOT A THING. Don't do that. We stained our clothes!

One friend wasn't used to wearing heels and she slid into the pie-coated floor and fell right down. "Don't worry," she said. "I broke the fall with my face."

Later, we all went onto my sister's roof. The sky was inky blue and starless, and the air crisp. Music from parties in other apartments drifted up to us. Her roof has no rail and is a dangerous place for drunk people retrieving their lost lives, but that's what we did. When someone tottered towards the edge, we nabbed them back. It was our own spontaneous New Year's ritual. It made New Year's not just a drunken bender, but a communal effort to become safely ourselves again.

Throw a New Year's or Any Time of the Year Lives Back party for you and your friends. Chances are they have some lives to retrieve from sadistic bosses, crazy exes, or problem teenagers.

Think of "Lives Back" as a cheer you are going to cheer all year long for yourself. Okay, everybody...

Lives Back
Lives Back
Lives Back!

remembering the beginning

We shall not cease from exploration, and the end of all our exploring will be to arrive where we started and know the place for the first time.

T. S. Eliot

Our memory shifts focus at different stages of our breakup. Sometimes it jumps back and forth between the good and the bad. Sometimes it creates a story that our partner was always the villain or always perfect and we miss everything about them.

In *All About Love*, bell hooks writes: "It is easier to articulate the pain of love's absence than to describe its presence and meaning in our lives." There will come a day, maybe even part of today, when you can muse about all the love you have in your life. Love for the earth, and its love for you, love of simple pleasures, love of your family and/or chosen family. I took a groovy workshop at a resort once, and it shifted my perspective on love. They taught us that you can, at any time, be in a room of love, a house of love, a neighborhood of love. It is just a subtle shift in perspective. You're in a room of love right now.

Goodbye for Now

THE PAST LOVES BUSH

The saddest thing about love, Joe, is that not only the love cannot last forever, but even the heartbreak is soon forgotten.

William Faulkner

The end never comes when you think it will. It's always ten steps past the worst moment, then a weird turn to the left.

Lena Dunham

I took myself on a holiday to Calistoga, a mineral bath and wine-tasting haven in Northern California. I had a massage gift certificate to use and my aunt would be visiting from Southern California (in an RV!). But it would be just me in my hotel room and I was pleased that I felt content about that. I parked in a nondescript lot to find a café in which to write. A big wooden planter on the cement caught my eye. It said, *"I want less…"* Intrigued, I walked over and saw that the big plant was covered with orange tags that said what people wanted less of, things like *"racism," "terrorism," "Trump."* Someone wanted *"Less hate and more acceptance and less school pls."*

I noticed that there was one more planter. It said, *"Past Loves…"* I turned over the tags to see what people had written about past loves:

Dad I love you
I no you have a wife now I naw [exact spelling]
Uncle Archie

My current cheating husband
I love you then, today, forever (S- age 30)
Go fucking find yourself.

And this one:

Mr. X - Thank you for releasing me from your sickness/I forgive you and I too set you free

(I wondered if some of these, like the above one, should be prosecuted.)

And then:

To Noodle and Tomato my two kittens I will love you forever.

As I was reading the tags, a couple walked by with a dog. He was wearing black and she was wearing light summery clothes. He said, "I think the labyrinth always leads you to the center, no matter which way you take."

I read one more, *"My love it's been four years since you passed- and I still love you-but its time to move on. I know you want me to be happy so send me someone! Xoxo Samantha."* I was about to leave when I noticed there was also a Gratitude bush. I went to each planter and filled out a card and tied the little white strings in knots around the branches.

On the Past Loves bush, I put names of all my great loves, ending with my most recent ex. On the other side, I wrote that I was ready for my life partner, but that I was also content with being loving to myself and taking myself on getaways! I closed my eyes, and a magical wind blew over me, reminiscent of the wind that blows away all the lesser nannies in *Mary Poppins*, leaving only Ms. Poppins herself.

As I was putting my stuff in my car to leave, I saw an older man in a baseball cap watering Past Loves, sending all our wishes out into the world. So that's one more idea I leave you with. Find a tree or bush and adorn it with "Past Loves," "Gratitude," or any other phrase that helps you heal. Perhaps friends and family members can tie their tags on. Then like Tibetan prayer flags, your wishes can be sent on the winds, finding, perhaps, other wishes carried on recently blownout birthday candles and little dandelion stamens.

My favorite Shakespeare play is *A Midsummer Night's Dream.* It's a feast of fairies, blessings, spell casting, and magic drops that make people fall in love. And then at the end, it leaves you wondering, was it real or but a dream?

If we shadows have offended,
Think but this, and all is mended,
That you have but slumbered here
While these visions did appear...

At some point it may be helpful to think of your past relationship as a dream, even a beautiful dream in which you slumbered "while these visions did appear." This is the necessary fading of all things. Inherent in each event is its completion. On some level, all is a dream; a great, wondrous adventure that we tend to take too seriously. We fixate on what we don't have instead of exulting in what we possess. If that was a dream now passed, you can dream again into a present and future of your choosing. Instead of clinging, over time you can see that we are but dreamwalking from one world to the next.

Your friends might not always see things in this dreamy way. While you are in your healing space they may give you all kinds of crazy comments like: *When you stop looking, you will find your next love.* It's a Catch-22 summed up best by David Holmes:

I resigned myself to the fact that I wasn't going to meet a man at this place, partially because everyone tells you you meet your soulmate when you stop looking. But then, of course, the second you stop looking, you start thinking is this it? Is this when it's going to happen, now that I'm not looking? Which is its own insidious way of still looking. It's a vicious cycle.

no bummer future thinking

My dad's parental philosophies could be boiled down to these:

- Weed is the cure-all
- You can always drop out and join the hippie commune
- No Bummer Future Thinking

When I asked him what got him over breakups, he said: "Weed and time." It's a good tip since weed actually warps and morphs time. Then again, he said weed was good for menstrual cramps, insomnia, depression, avoiding feelings, any pain, appetite enhancement, the common cold (moves it right through), and a fever (it will help you sweat it right out). Nothing disappoints him more than the fact that none of his daughters blossomed into full-blown potheads. If we only applied ourselves…

If I was having a stressful time in a high school class, or I was unhappy in a social situation, he would always remind me that I could *drop out and join the hippie commune.* And I could. And in my way I have. I don't live communally (yet) but I live an artist's life. There are hippie communes you could join. Back to the land is always happening somewhere. If not in the US, try Sweden, Costa Rica, or India.

If my sisters and I worried about the future, Dad would caution us against Bummer Future Thinking. He reminded us that we didn't know what magical things were in store for us so why would we bum ourselves out by assuming the worst? Then he would hand us a joint, and we would remind him for the hundredth time that we didn't smoke, that we were under the age of twelve, and that we had to leave for school in a few moments. So take his advice with a grain of ganja, but I think he was on to something. This is no time to languish in Bummer Future Thinking. I don't know about you, but I'm going to be wringing out my sponges, because what if Jennifer Lawrence (J Law!) totally wants to date me? Or you? You never know.

every single **breath**

Remember way back in the beginning of the book when my first love asked why I "stopped loving" him? Here is an abbreviated version of what I wrote:

You were my first true love so I have at many times examined our relationship for clues about who I am and what love is. You loved me very well. And I was crazy about you and crazy in love with you. As I am sure you have noticed there are many assholes out there. You were such a gentleman and such a lover and such a wonderful first love.

So the short answer is nothing. Nothing made me stop loving you. I continued to love you for years after we broke up. Almost an obsessive love. I broke up with you mainly because I was too young to have found the one. I knew intuitively I had so much to explore: travel, bisexuality, so many roads, lovers, relationships, growth.

After that we continued reminiscing. Through this process I was reminded that I was the one who destroyed the love of the first person who truly loved me. Or at least that's one way to tell the story. It's been a real come-to-Isis time for me. It was a messy breakup.

In our correspondence he wrote: *Do you remember when we reconnected after a year or so of being broken up and I spent the night at your place? I would have loved to be back with you but you kicked me out the next morning. Broke my poor heart again.* Reading this broke my poor heart again.

Maybe this book is a way for me to make amends. And to make peace with that young teenage girl who was testing the boundaries and limits of love. She was a really sweet girl. But she did some hurtful things.

Well, it's goodbye for now. We can reconnect on the internet via www.aprilhirschman.com. Open the pages of this book any time you want to come back into the Temple of Healing. I'll leave you with what I say to all my buddies in the throes of a breakup:

The best is yet to come.

BONUS SECTION

RECIPES: THE **HEART HEALING** KITCHEN

Hello and welcome to your coping cuisine! Sometimes when I haven't cooked in a while, I set up my kitchen with some atmosphere. I light a candle, put on some music, and clean off the counter, transforming my kitchen into an inviting space. Since cooking for oneself is the ultimate act of self-love, here are some inspiring concoctions to delight your senses. I am an Amelia Bedelia cook (I put in "a little of this and little of that") so these recipes are really jumping-off points for your imagination.

Morning Drinks

Smoothing-Out-the-Rough-Edges Smoothie

Vegan, gluten-free, caffeine-free

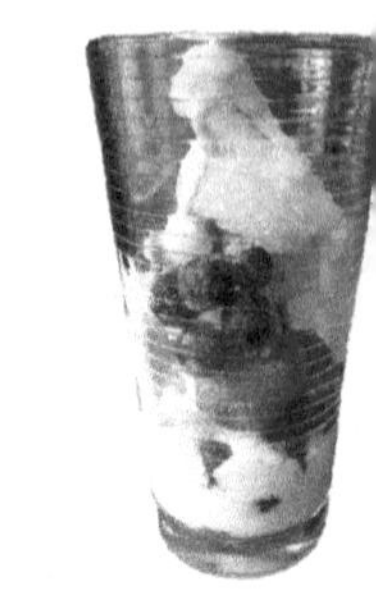

¾ to 1 cup almond milk
1 teaspoon almond butter
half a banana
1 teaspoon coconut oil
a pinch of cinnamon
1 teaspoon of vanilla
1 scoop pea or brown rice protein
optional: 1 date

Mix It Up:
Pour almond milk in first. Play with thickness by adding more or less almond milk. Then add all other ingredients and blend.

All-Day-Long Drinks

Virgin Aloe Vera Margaritas

Vegan, gluten-free, caffeine-free

½ cup Aloe Vera juice or gel (the drinking kind, not the skin kind)
½ cup water
1 leaf kale
1 tablespoon fresh lime juice
honey to taste
4 ice cubes

Mix It Up:
Blend this concoction. Makes just over one cup. Garnish with mint and a slice of lime.
Midnight Margaritas!
I don't add tequila, as I like to keep the mind clear for the fever of creation.

Nightcaps: Heart Healing Tea Infusions

Having a warm, mildly sweet drink to sip before bed is a great nightly ritual treat.

The Balm!

Vegan, gluten-free, caffeine-free

The lovely green leaves of the lemon balm plant reside in the mint family. It is said to increase appetite, lessen anxiety and stress, and help with digestion.

Motherwort, hawthorn, and rose petals all have heart healing properties. Play with the amounts of motherwort, hawthorn, rose petals, and lemon balm.

Try ½ teaspoon of each
2 cups of water

Mix It Up:
Put the above herbs into your favorite teapot.
Boil the water. Pour into the pot. Let steep five minutes.

Golden Milk

Vegan, gluten- free, caffeine-free

You can buy golden milk powder (Gaia herbs) and just mix it in your nut or dairy milk of choice. Another option is this recipe:

1 ½ cups almond milk
1 teaspoon turmeric
a shake or two of black pepper
Play with amounts of ingredients below:
a pinch to a ¼ teaspoon of each
garam masala
cardamom powder
cinnamon and nutmeg

Optional: 1 teaspoon coconut oil
Optional: 1 date for sweetness

Mix it Up:

1)Simmer all ingredients (except date) 8 to 10 minutes. It will lose some liquid so add more if needed.
2)Add honey or 1 date.
3)You can leave it at that or blend in a blender to further combine the herbs and add one date if you want it more sweet. Make sure you remove the pit.

Top with nutmeg.
For an iced version, blend the above ingredients in a blender with some ice cubes.

Passionflower and Mulungu

Vegan, gluten-free, caffeine-free

Passionflower is said to aid sleep and reduce anxiety and circular thinking. Mulungu is said to calm the nervous system and help with anxiety. As always, check with your doctor before trying a new herb.

1 or 2 teaspoons of passionflower and mulungu mix
1 ½ cups milk of choice
Optional: Honey and cinnamon to taste.

Mix It Up:
Stir 1 or 2 teaspoons of the powder into nut or dairy milk. Heat in a pot or microwave.
If you have a foaming wand, this works great to mix.
Optional: honey to taste and some cinnamon
Twisted Thistle has a great blend.
www.twistedthistleapothecary.com

Masala Chai for Sensitive People

Vegan, caffeine-free, sugar-free

I've been making my own Chai for ages now. It's always a little different but always well received. I took a Chai class in Varkala, India, where the teacher smashed the cardamom pods with the flat end of the knife to release the fragrance. Here is my adaptation based on what I learned and my own experiments.

3 cardamom pods broken open by pressing a knife into them or 1 teaspoon powdered cardamom
a shake of cinnamon
3 slices of ginger, chopped up any which way
about 6 black peppercorns
a shake of nutmeg
a shake of ashwagandha (optional)
a handful of fennel seeds or two anise stars
1 cup nut or dairy milk (I like half almond, half coconut creamer, unsweetened)
¾ cup water to boil
1 dandelion tea bag, or scoop of reishi mushroom roast,* or rooibos, or decaf (or caffeinated black tea bag)
honey to taste
** Can be purchased at www.farmacopia.com.*

1) Bring water to a boil.
2) Simmer it with ginger and cardamom pods for 10 minutes. Make sure you don't run out of water. May need to add more.
3) Add the rest of the ingredients. I like to have a more creamy Chai. Play with the ratio of water and milk to get your desired consistency. Turn up the heat to medium.
4) Bring to a boil so the foam reaches the top of the pot. Then turn down heat. Repeat this three more times.
5) Strain into your favorite mug. Shake some nutmeg on top for garnish.

If it's too watery just add more cold milk into the warm beverage. If you are in a hurry, you can just simmer everything together. Makes about 1 cup. Double for two and you can also store some for the next day.

April's Heart Heal Jook

Vegan, gluten-free

Jook or Congee is a delicious Asian rice porridge that goes down really easy and has a bouquet of aromatic condiments to give it flavor. In Japan on January 7th they eat this to recover from the holidays, protect from evil, and fortify the body against illness. The best part is this meal can last up to 4-5 days because the toppings are kept separate. Jook easily reheats on the stove or microwave; just add some water.

This recipe requires a bit of tending and stirring and adding water. Think of it as a healing potion. Imagine you are stirring up a new, happy, self-loving life. With each ingredient, say what it means to your life. More spice with the ginger, more money with the broccoli, etc.
If you want to get super witchy about it, sing:

Make for yourself a power spot
Bring you a spoon and a cooking pot
Bring air bring fire bring water bring earth
And you a new Universe will birth.
And you a new Universe will birth!

-Shekhinah Mountainwater

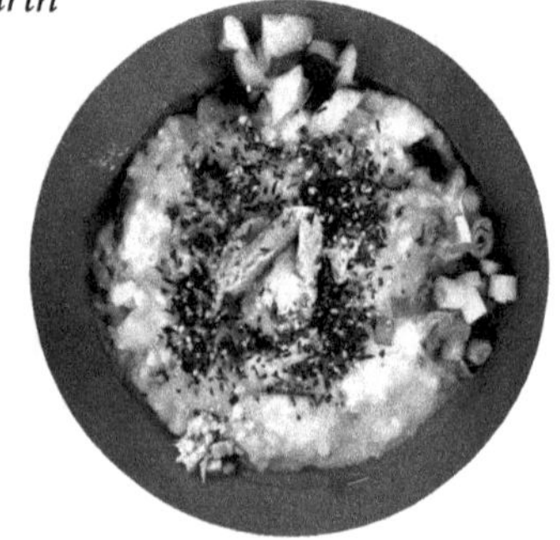

1 cup uncooked Jasmine or Basmati white rice (I tried it with brown and it was dreary)
2 cups vegetable broth, bone broth, or other stock
2 cups water
1 inch fresh ginger, finely diced
two carrots cut into moons
4 fresh shitake mushrooms
1 small bunch of broccolini cut diagonally into 1 inch pieces
pinch of pink Himalayan salt
several cups of water to add as needed
two handfuls of spinach

Toppings

You definitely need some toppings but you don't need ALL of these. See what combinations appeal to you. Choose at least one sauce, one pungent green (onion or cilantro), and one protein.

two stalks chopped green onions
chopped handful of cilantro
kimchee
soy sauce or coconut aminos
sesame oil
protein topping options: My favorite is a can of good wild sockeye salmon because the oiliness flavors the dish. You could also do baked chicken, raw or baked tofu, or tempeh.
avocado slices
diced cucumber
peanuts, raw or roasted
furikake or dulce flakes
grated fresh ginger

Mix It Up:

1. Wash the rice. Put rice, stock, and 2 cups of water into a large pot and bring to a boil. Once it boils, turn the temperature down to medium low to simmer. Simmer for 20 minutes and add ginger.
2. Simmer for 10 more minutes and add carrots, mushrooms and salt.

3. Simmer for another 15 to 30 minutes, adding water as necessary to maintain a thick oatmeal consistency. Make sure the bottom does not brown or burn.
4. When the jook is almost a velvety porridge consistency, add broccoli florets.
5. Stir in the spinach 1 minute before serving.

Snacks!

California Cottage

Contains dairy; gluten-free

When I was a kid summering at the Sands Beach Club on Long Island, the older Jewish ladies in my family would always get the diet plate for lunch. It was usually fruit and cottage cheese. It always had too much melon. Ever notice how melon can make you sad sometimes? For some reason in the 1980s, eating cottage cheese meant that you were on a diet.

I am pretty proud of this little concoction I came up with and it's much better than those dreary diet plates. This makes a great small meal or hearty snack. No cooking involved! Just a wee bit of slicing. Did you know avocados contain more potassium than bananas? And cucumbers are a great source of pantothenic acid, whatever that is! It's good for you! Science!

1 ½ cups cottage cheese
2 small diced Persian cucumbers
1 ½ tablespoons good olive oil
A couple shakes of furikake or dulce flakes
Fresh ground pepper (must be fresh ground!)
1 small or half of a large avocado diced.

Mix It Up:
Mix the above ingredients and then gently mix in the avocado. Play with the amounts of ingredients. You might like it densely

packed with cukes and avo or you may like those to just be hinted at. Serve yourself a bowl and then put leftovers in small snack containers for later. If you are going to keep it past 2 days, don't add the avocado and instead keep adding fresh ones to the mix with each serving.

Hippie Popcorn Party

Vegan, gluten-free

I'll never forget the day my friend's mom sprinkled nutritional yeast on our popcorn and we sat down to watch *Jason and the Argonauts*. A culinary star was born. Fortified nutritional yeast even contains iron and B12, and is a complete protein!

1-3 tablespoons of coconut oil
¼ to ⅓ cup of Hippie Dust (aka nutritional yeast.) The more golden yellow the better. Get the flakey one, not the powdery kind.
Organic popcorn

Mix It Up:

1) Coat the bottom of a pot with oil. If you have a glass lid, use that; if not, any lid will do. I eyeball the amount of kernels. It depends on how much you want to make. You will probably make too much; it's just the nature of popcorn.
2) So once you have decided on an amount, pour the kernels into the bottom.
3) Heat up to medium and shake the pan around until you hear that glorious popping sound. If you do make too much, throw it away that night! There is nothing sadder than eating stale popcorn or having it stare at you from the counter.
4) Heat up the butter until melted. If using oil, no need to heat. Mix the yeast into the butter. Adjust amounts until it's a pourable paste. Pour over popcorn. Pour a couple more shakes of the yeast. Et voilà!

Books To Read When Hiding Under A Blanket

Simple Abundance, Sarah Ban Breathnach
Perfect Love, Imperfect Relationships, John Welwood
The Invitation, Oriah
The Alchemist, Paulo Coelho
Pronoia, Rob Brezsney
The Life Changing Magic of Tidying Up, Marie Kondo
The Artist's Way, Julia Cameron
Magick Tarot, Magick Altman
The New Diary, Tristine Rainer
When Things Fall Apart &
Comfortable with Uncertainty, Pema Chödrön

Movies to Watch When Trapped Under Boxes of Takeout Food

Marilyn Monroe: *Gentlemen Prefer Blondes, Some Like it Hot, How to Marry a Millionaire*
Rita Hayworth: *Gilda*
Katherine Hepburn and Cary Grant: *Holiday*
Bill Murray: *Meatballs, Scrooged, Tootsie*
The Big Lebowski
Notting Hill
Girls Just Want to Have Fun
Amelie
Bridesmaids
An Unmarried Woman
Love, Valor, Compassion
The Intervention
High Fidelity
Singin' in the Rain

Television

Ally McBeal
Murder, She Wrote
Absolutely Fabulous
The Bold Type
The Marvelous Mrs. Maisel
Younger

Resource Guide:

April's Offerings

www.aprilhirschman.com

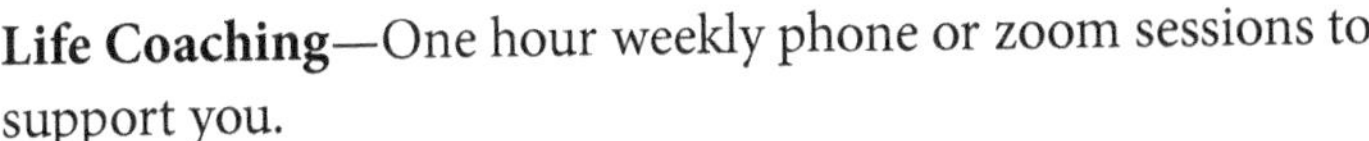

Life Coaching—One hour weekly phone or zoom sessions to support you.
Tarot Readings—One hour ten card reading checking in on your life through the wisdom and symbolism of the Tarot.
Speaking Engagements—Presentations on breakup recovery, removing obstacles to success, and living out loud.

Grief.com (great website with resources for books, groups, and videos about grief)
Suicide Hotline 1-800-273-8255
Acupuncture Sage Staggs: www.sagestaggs.com
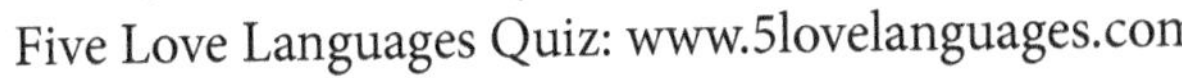
Herbs, Oracles, and Crystals: www.twistedthistleapothecary.com
Five Love Languages Quiz: www.5lovelanguages.com

Thanks Ever So!

Thanks to Kelly Gillease, who takes me to the ballet, and was the first one to dance her eyes along these words when they were still in their toddler stage. Meaningful glances at Kate Sims for reading with her big brain focus and writing little hearts next to what she liked! Dara Sklar was a huge champion of this book and even discussed it with me poolside while the naked gay men of a Russian River resort sunbathed around us. She reminded me that the reader needed to feel safe inside this book. Jay Bordon, Rachel Averbuck, and Yair Harel jumped in with some great edits. Skylar Young spent oodles of hours beaming her brilliant mind on this. Miss you Sky Sky. I can hear your laughter all the way from the Bay. I'll do the parallel parking, I promise! Shannon O'Malley is a magnificent writer who helped me shape this book and encouraged its humor. Susyn Reeve is on the heart-healing writer's path too, and shined her light on my words. To Esther Baruch, my editor, for rooting out anything divisive or too zany and putting the polish on. To all my friends who have listened to me talk about my imaginary friends (writing projects): look everyone, this one is REAL! Very appreciative of stand-up comics whom I have quoted frequently in this book; laughter makes the bitter sweet! Chelsea Price and all the women of Twisted Thistle Apothecary who added their philosophical and herbal wisdom to this. Sage Staggs for sharing her acupuncture wisdom. Jane McDonough gave me some great reflections on what was working. Angelo Festin and Yanika Schneider for getting on public transit with knives and pots and coming over to my place for recipe testing, food photos, and feasting!

I so appreciate Sofia Limón whose keen eye, creativity, and patience brought the design of this book into its glorious finality!

I had the joy of reconnecting with cousin Amy Solomon and her encouragement helped me move forward. I won the family lottery! You all inspire me to pieces and mieces and geeses. Thanks to my sister Celeste for great edits and Allegra for Everybody, Lives Back and overall wonderfulness. Dear sisters, you are some of the favorite voices in my head. Thanks to my pops for No Bummer Future Thinking and other philosophical nuggets. Endless gratitude to my mom who gave me notes, Tarot wisdom, and kept saying: "Get it out there!"

photo by Lydia Daniller

April Hirschman is a Life Coach, filmmaker, yoga instructor, belly dancer, tarot reader, artist, amateur stand-up comedian, and one of the 10 Priestesses you should know in the 21st century! Her writing has appeared in *New Moon Magazine for Girls* and *Common Ground Magazine.* Her short films have won awards and screened internationally. She smoked her first vape with Armistead Maupin, and put on her makeup with John Cameron Mitchell. She lives in San Francisco.

CPSIA information can be obtained
at www.ICGtesting.com
Printed in the USA
FSHW021806050519
57864FS